DATE DUE

Eisenstein: Three Films

Eisenstein: Three Films

Edited by Jay Leyda

Translated by Diana Matias

Battleship Potemkin · October
Alexander Nevsky

Icon Editions

Harper & Row, Publishers

New York, Evanston, San Francisco, London

Eisenstein: Three Films copyright © 1974 by Lorrimer Publishing Limited

FIRST US EDITION

ISBN: 0-06-430055-2 (paper) 0-06-432975-5 (cloth)

LIBRARY OF CONGRESS CATALOG CARD NUMBER: 74-6548

CONTENTS

A NOTE ON THIS EDITION

The following texts and notes are based on various published and manuscript sources. Eisenstein's habit of keeping almost all his work materials is an unusual benefit to the students of his films. The richness of his archive should, however, prepare the reader of the following documents for unexpected additional manuscripts and information. According to the most recent published research on *Potemkin* and *October* it is possible that more complete texts may yet be found for those films. The publishers can claim only that this volume represents the state of our information as of early 1974.

For the reader who wishes to check these translations against authoritative Russian texts the best current collection to consult is Volume VI (1971) of *Izbranniye proizvedeniya v shesti tomakh,* a collection of Eisenstein's writings that will be continued in the near future.

The publishers and editor acknowledge the help given them by the Central Archive (TZGALI), the Eisenstein Kabinet, Gosfilmofond (all in Moscow), the National Film Archive (London), and the Museum of Modern Art (New York City).

INTRODUCTION

by Jay Leyda

" . . . by Eisenstein." This is as clear and acknowledged a statement of authorship as we can find in film history thus far. Only the signatures of Chaplin, of Bergman, of Dreyer, of Méliès, of Dovzhenko similarly carry the weight of their claims beyond dispute. But this volume contains a fact — three facts! — throwing the " sole authorship " of these three scenarios back into the argument. In each of these scenarios Eisenstein had a writer-collaborator: For *Battleship Potemkin* it was Nina Agadzhanova, co-author of the anniversary scenario *1905*, where the mutiny on the *Potemkin* was one of many episodes it was thought necessary to reconstruct for such a film; to the end of his life Eisenstein never ceased to show his gratitude to " Nuna's " contribution to *Battleship Potemkin*. In preparing the anniversary film of *October* there is no doubt that Eisenstein and Alexandrov collaborated on the scenario (published herein), though no one was in any doubt who contributed its boldest invention and imagery. The initiative for *Alexander Nevsky* came from its co-author, Pyotr Pavlenko, without whose dramatic experience and political reliability Eisenstein could not even have started its production; and who will say that Prokofiev's score could have been replaced by another composer's with the same powerful effect?

In this delicate matter of a film's authorship, where it is normal for even the truest *auteur* to have a hundred collaborators at all stages of production, I believe that artistic control — authorship — can be traced (at least in those films that have not been merely manufactured) to a single controlling mind. Sergei Gerasimov, in an interview of 1964, put it unequivocally:

> In my view the author is the one who intellectually dominates the ensemble. It can be the writer, the director, the cameraman, the actor. It is always the one who is the real master of the initial idea and of the *passions* of the work. The one who literally dominates

7

the others. . . .[1]

" Dominates " is a word easily associated with Eisenstein's character, certainly as it showed itself in the process of creation, whether of an invention, a staging plan, or a film. Yet one of the most basic of the dominated elements, the dramatic framework, was always provided by another mind, with the eventual collaboration of the " master ". Eisenstein's only film for which he was the sole scenarist was *Ivan the Terrible*, and that was a job of writing that he approached alone with great reluctance, finally dependent on historical facts, enormous research and a quantity of hidden purposes that would have been difficult to conceal from a collaborator. In the seeming contradiction between his mastery and someone else's dramatic scaffolding, Eisenstein is not unique. In their plays (though not in their poetry) playwrights as diverse as Brecht and Eliot required the support of a provided frame. Perhaps a musician can improvise more freely on a given theme.

" Scenario " is a word of several meanings, describing the several ways the plan of a staged performance can be set down on paper. Of the three scenarios in this volume, only the third, for *Alexander Nevsky*, resembles forms still in international use, the " screenplay" or "treatment" (called in Soviet practice the "literary version"). The step between treatment and finished film is the " shooting script", and the *October* script published here outlines the material to be shot (for a *silent* film, in this case), leaving plenty of room for change and expansion in the process of actual filming. The scenario for *Potemkin*, however, is an " emergency " script: in the midst of production an earlier script (for *1905*) has been discarded, and all the new thoughts have to be set down on paper, for the sake of both crew (in Odessa) and administration (in Moscow); it embodies some material that has been shot and ideas not yet filmed. At this stage radical alterations can be made in the filming as well as during the cutting. In the endless arguments whether to prepare a film loosely or tightly (the so-called " iron scenario " usually taught at film schools), *Potemkin* is often mentioned as an example of a film made without a scenario, but this script was found

---

[1] In *Cinema in Revolution*, a collection of statements published in Great Britain by Martin Secker & Warburg, and in the United States by Hill & Wang, 1973, p. 121.

among Eisenstein's papers and published (for the first time in 1956) to show that this masterpiece also required paper work.

In all three scenarios, and especially in *Potemkin*, the reader should not be surprised to discover that certain memorable moments and images are missing, having found their way into the finished films later, even at the last moment. The " iron scenario " is no more than a plan, and the realization of a film's plan encounters many unexpected factors and intuitions that the film-maker would be foolish to ignore. Unsurprising, too, are the ideas in the original plan that are discarded in the filming or in the editing. The boiling political situation at the time of the tenth anniversary of the October Revolution could not leave the anniversary film, *October*, untouched, and the finished film does not follow its plan — there were too many powerful cooks watching over that dish. More through accident than intention, one entire reel of *Nevsky* was dropped from the finished film[1] — it can be read in the scenario.

Some film records are published as " scenarios " that have nothing to do with a film's preparation. More accurately these are " shot-lists ", notations of the shots and sounds of finished films. They have their uses, and the chances for survival are better than those of preparatory scripts. Shot-lists are often required for copyright purposes or by boards of censors (for example, the *Protokol* published by German censors); an original script that has disappeared can be replaced by transcribing a shot-list from the finished film (Dovzhenko himself supplied missing scripts in this way — and enjoyed it!). On several occasions *Potemkin* shot-lists (rarely identical) have been published in various languages. But a genuine scenario, in any form, gives us valuable information about the creative process — especially when the finished film is also available — that no post facto recording can provide. When there is a choice, as between the scenario or shot-list of Part II of *Ivan the Terrible*, there could be an ulterior motive in choosing to publish the shot-list.

Another recent type of recording moves even further away from information about the process. This is the *dia-positive* or slide-film, that appears to be an attempt to replace films with stills — for " study purposes "! There is more excuse, and less expense, in the

---

[1] See *Sight & Sound*, Spring 1965, p. 63; see also, below, p. 143.

recently introduced *microfiche*. But nothing can replace the film itself, and the work materials related to its production, in investigating the nature and accomplishment of a film.

J.L.

BATTLESHIP POTEMKIN

Eisenstein's successful first film, *Strike,* was shown publicly on April 28, 1925, just as the committee appointed to celebrate the twentieth anniversary of the 1905 Revolution was deciding which anniversary films were to be made by whom. Two 1905 subjects were already in production but the success of *Strike* brought the biggest project to Eisenstein and the scenarist Nina Agadzhanova — *The Year 1905.* Eisenstein had left Proletcult, for whom *Strike* had been made, and the other films in the planned cycle on pre-revolutionary action had been put aside. He had wanted to make his next film with Isaac Babel, but the anniversary proposal took precedence. The committee's decision was made in June, the scenario was ready by early July, when filming began in Leningrad and Moscow.

The deadline for the completed film was the last week of December (when the official celebration would take place). When the crew grew worried that the un-summer-like weather in the north would delay their shooting schedule, they changed their plan and hurried south to film episodes on the Black Sea, including the mutiny on the battleship *Prince Potemkin of Tauride.* It was a decision that changed the course of film history.

In the 900 shots planned for *The Year 1905,* forty-four shots* were to reconstruct the mutiny in June-July 1905 of the *Potemkin*'s sailors and the support given them by the people of Odessa. However, when the crew reached Odessa, the original plan and the scenario of *1905* were replaced by a new plan and a hastily drafted scenario that was to rely upon the *Potemkin*-Odessa sequence, to make the entire anniversary film shorter and sharper.

Eisenstein never denied that it was his first sight of the Odessa Steps that changed the direction of the film: " No scene of shooting on the Odessa Steps appeared in any of the preliminary versions or in any of the montage lists that were prepared [before filming began]. It was born in the instant of immediate contact."† In the same memoir he wrote, "The Odessa Steps became the decisive scene at the very spine of the film." It was the first sequence to be written for the new script.

In a more detailed analysis, also written long after the fact, Eisenstein told how he gravitated to a nearly classic five-act form, even to giving titles to each of the " acts ":

      I, Men and Maggots
      II, Drama on the Quarterdeck

---

* The fragment of the *1905* scenario is given in the appendix below.
† Written in 1945, " The Birth of a Film," *The Hudson Review* (New York), Summer 1951. This memoir is surprisingly full of accidents and improvisations during the production of *Battleship Potemkin.*

III, Appeal from the Dead
IV, The Odessa Steps
  V, Meeting the Squadron*

Even though the implicit outline of this precise structure can be found in the four parts of the " shooting script " given below, it requires an effort to identify the unforgettable details of the finished film with the script, the exact date of which is not known, but it is clear from the corrections that its composition continued during the actual shooting that began at the end of August.

The December deadline was met, incredibly. The long and complicated career of " the most powerful film " had begun.

---

* Published in 1939 " The Structure of the Film," in *Film Form* (New York, 1949, 1957, 1969). Sergei Tretyakov collaborated on the text of these and all other sub-titles in the film.

BATTLESHIP POTEMKIN

The script published here is the director's shooting script, which was produced by Eisenstein late in 1925 on the basis of what was originally a single episode in the *1905* scenario (see appendix). It represents a particular stage in Eisenstein's work on the film and an effort has been made to reproduce the form of the original typescript as closely as possible. Eisenstein's handwritten insertions and additions are therefore printed in italics.

The film titles did not yet exist in their final version and in most cases the script simply indicates their position and approximate content. These indications were either typed in capital letters or set off in box frames by Eisenstein himself, and that style has been retained here.

The editorial notes in the Russian edition of this script are retained here as footnotes. Text appearing between square parentheses has been added by the translator for clarity.

Technical terms are used in full in the first instance and in abbreviated form thereafter, as follows: **close-up (CU)**; medium shot (MS); long shot (LS).

*   *   *

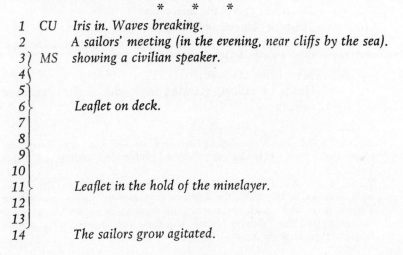

```
 1    CU    Iris in. Waves breaking.
 2           A sailors' meeting (in the evening, near cliffs by the sea).
 3 ⎫  MS    showing a civilian speaker.
 4 ⎬
 5 ⎫
 6 ⎬         Leaflet on deck.
 7 ⎪
 8 ⎭
 9 ⎫
10 ⎪
11 ⎬         Leaflet in the hold of the minelayer.
12 ⎪
13 ⎭
14           The sailors grow agitated.
```

15

1(15)[1]		The officer of the watch. In the background, sailors gathered around hanging sides of meat.
2(16)	CU	Officer.
3		From above: sailors with the meat. (Still)
4		The officer walks off.
5		Indignant sailors seen past the hanging meat.
6	CU	Sailors peeling potatoes.
7	CU	Sailors washing cabbage.
8	CU	Heads of sailors, talking vociferously.
9		As above.
10	CU	Peeling potatoes.
11	CU	Sailors' heads.
12	CU	Cabbage.
13		Agitated sailors. The ship's doctor and the officer come up.
1		The hanging meat.
2		The doctor removes his pince-nez.
3	CU	Hands folding pince-nez.
4	CU	Eye, folded eye-pieces are brought up to the eye.
5	CU	Worms in the meat, seen through the pince-nez.
6	CU	Gesticulating with his pince-nez the doctor speaks: — These are the dead larvae of flies. They're harmless — they can be washed off with brine.
7		Angry sailors' faces.
1a[2]		The officer drives the men away.
1b		The men disperse unwillingly.
1c		The officer leaves. In the background, sailors dispersing.
2	MS	Ship's cooks hack up the meat.
3	CU	Meat being chopped.
4		Heads of sailors, glancing in at the engine room and talking.

---

[1] Breaks in the frame numbering are due to the fact that Eisenstein elaborated these episodes at different intervals, adding to them gradually.

[2] Where a particular frame number has been extended by the letters a, b, etc., as in this case, the additional frames are those inserted by Eisenstein in the course of re-working existing texts. In the original manuscript of the " Odessa Steps " sequence, such frames were written into the typescript by hand.

5	A cauldron boils.
6	Sailors cleaning the muzzle of the ship's gun and talking.
7	The cauldron boiling.
8	?[1] Sailors talking.
9	The meat being thrown into the cauldron.
10	The meat being hacked.
11	The cauldron bubbling.
12	*Dissolve to seething faces of the sailors.*
12	Signal for the meal.
13	An officer goes into the men's mess.
14	Empty tables.
14a	The officer looks [at the empty tables].
15	Untouched bowls.

16]
17}   *Sailors chewing bread etc. in various corners of the*
18| *battleship.*
19]

| 20 | Sailors buying food at the ship's canteen. An officer passes. Hostile eyes follow him. |
| 21 | The officer in the kitchen. The cook tells him the men won't accept the soup. |

22]
23}   *Sailors chewing food.*
24]

25	The officer issues an order.
26	Drums roll.
27	The crew forms ranks on both sides of the quarter-deck.
28	The commander comes out onto the capstan.
29		*Threat*[2]	
30	Sombre faces of the sailors.
31	The commander points menacingly towards the masthead.
32	Sailors look sombrely at the masthead.
33	Masthead — dissolve — sailors' bodies hanging [from the yardarm], double exposure.
34	Bitter faces of the sailors.

---

[1] Left blank in the original.

[2] This is a brief indication of the sense of the title proposed at this point.

35		The commander gives an order.
36		STEP FORWARD THOSE WHO ARE PREPARED TO EAT THE SOUP.
37		Two sailors confer.
38	MS	The petty officers step briskly forward.
39		One sailor starts to move but another restrains him.
40	LS	Shot from above of large group of sailors moving over to the gun turret.
41	MS	Gilerovsky[1] watches them and counts. He is standing next to the commander.
42	MS	A group of sailors crossing over.
43		Gilerovsky has finished counting. He gives an order.
44		Bewilderment among the remaining sailors.
45		Agitation among those who have crossed over.
46		Officers Gilerovsky and Levintsov[2] bar the way between the two groups.
47		Gilerovsky gives an order.
48		The guards take two steps forward and raise their rifles.
49		Gilerovsky gives an order.
49a			TARPAULIN	
50		The sailors at the gun turret stagger back.
51		The petty officers run up.
52		The tarpaulin drops on the condemned sailors. *(Still)*
53		The sailors shudder.
53a		A black-robed priest holding a crucifix.
53b		*Eagle on the prow of the* Potemkin.
54		Motionless officer.
55		
55a		The petty officers stand to attention.
56		Gilerovsky narrows his eyes.
56a		*The group under the tarpaulin.*
57		The ship's cannon (to be replaced).[3]

---

[1] *Gilerovsky:* documentary sources and the titles of the finished film give the surname of the senior officer (whose role was played by G. V. Alexandrov) as "Gilyarovsky". In the text published here, this and other surnames are reproduced in the form in which they appear in the author's original.

[2] *Levintsov* (Liventsov): an officer of the *Prince Potemkin-Tavrichevsky*.

[3] This direction (see also frame 67) may be interpreted in two ways. It

58		The masthead (where the men were hanging).[1]
59		Smoke pours from the ship's funnel over the side.
59a	LS	*The battleship in calm seas and bright sunshine.*
60		The flag of St Andrew, barely lifting.
61		A flock of seagulls fly over the calm water.
61a[2]		
62		Dolphins leaping.
63		The surface of the tarpaulin, panning shot of sailors' legs [seen below it].
63a		The guards' guns waver.
64	CU	Vakulenchuk's head rises into shot. He looks, and shouts:
65		BROTHERS, WHY ARE YOU FORSAKING US?
66		The mast.
67		Cannon. (To be replaced.)
68	CU	The flag flutters furiously in the wind.
69	MS	The officer bends forward and watches.
70		
71		Frantic movement among the sailors near the gun turret.
71a		
72		Gilerovsky angrily gives an order. *(Still)*
73		The guards raise their rifles.
74		Faces of the guards, frowning, clenching their teeth.
75		The guards abruptly lower their rifles (no faces, and less depth than in 73).
76		Dolphins leaping.
77	CU	Gilerovsky.
78		Gilerovsky springs up and seizes a rifle from one of the guards.
79		The sailors near the gun turret scatter.
80		Vakulenchuk jumps up onto the gun turret and shouts.
81		Sailors breaking into the armoury.

---

either indicates the need to re-shoot existing shots of the guns; or to build a set of the kind of gun tower which existed on the *Potemkin*. (The battleship *Twelve Apostles,* on which the filming was carried out, no longer functioned as a warship but as a floating ammunition store.)

[1] The direction is imprecise in the manuscript — it relates back to the image of the condemned sailors (see frame 33 above).

[2] "Eagle on the prow of the *Potemkin*" was inserted here and then crossed out.

82		Gilerovsky catches sight of Vakulenchuk and gives chase.
83		Sailors strip the gun racks.
84		They break down the door of the armoury.
85		The petty officers run down to the hatchways.
85a		The men break open cases of bayonets, using knives and bare hands. Their hands bleed.
86		Vakulenchuk running, with Gilerovsky after him.
87		A sailor swings a gun at an officer, misses and breaks the gun.
87a		Sailors run up on deck.
88		Gilerovsky shoots. Vakulenchuk falls.
88a		The shot [Vakulenchuk] seen from above.
89		Sailors leap onto the officers.
90		A blow knocks the priest down a ladder. His crucifix is sent flying.
91		The ship's doctor is killed, the sailors toss him overboard. *(Still)*
92		His pince-nez catch on a cable.
93		A sailor strikes Gilerovsky in the back.
93a		Smoke pours out of the funnel. *See* 59
94		Gilerovsky is thrown overboard.
95		Gilerovsky clings to a rope.
96		I'LL GET YOU, YOU SCUM.
97	CU	Gilerovsky's face.
98	CU	Pince-nez dangling from the cable.
99		A gun shot.
100		Gilerovsky falls into the water.
101		Dissolve to sailors running to the dead Vakulenchuk.
102		Dissolve to whale-boat moving across the water with the body of Vakulenchuk (travelling shot).
103[1]		

---

[1] The following frames, numbered 103-109, and those immediately after them, 196-202, have been crossed out here. The content of frames 103-109 is worked out in detail in the opening of the next episode. The elaboration of frames 196-202 is not given at this point in the script. See footnote below, p. 25.

		The body of the dead sailor, Vakulenchuk
1	CU	A tent.
2	LS	Deserted mole, and the tent.
3		Dissolve to folded hands holding a candle.
4		Feet seen under a covering flag.
5		[Vakulenchuk's] head. *(Still)*
6	CU	Candle.
7		The funeral ribbon.
8		The *Potemkin*.
9		Anglers.
10		Floats in the water.
11		Anchor buoys.
12		Seagulls on the water.
13	MS	The mole with the tent.
14		Odessa from the sea.
15	LS	The mole with the tent. A few curious onlookers.
16		Dissolve to more people.
17		Dissolve to more still.
18		Dissolve to more still.
19 20 21 22		Crowds descending the Levashevsky steps.
23 24		Crowds stream down Market Street. *(Still)*
25 26		The crowd streaming down the harbour — seen through the ships. *(Still)*
27	LS	(From the London Restaurant).[1] Crowds of people gathering.
28		From inside the tent. People gathered around Vakulenchuk.
29		Two workers with heads bared.
30		Two peasant women kneel.
31		TEXT OF LEAFLET.
32		People kiss Vakulenchuk's head.

---

[1] Indicates the camera position. The film crew lived at the London Hotel.

33	A group watching with fixed attention.
34	Coins dropped into a cap [at the back of the tent].
35	An intellectual (Brodsky).
36	Two ladies with parasols.
37	An old man (Protopopov).
38	A young man reads the leaflet aloud.
39	An old worker takes notes on a scrap of paper.
40	A journalist takes notes in a notebook.
41	Two women singing.
42	Three workers singing. *(Still)*
43	One woman singing.
44	Two women kneel down and touch their foreheads to the ground.
45	A woman cries aloud.
46	A worker singing.
47	Several workers singing.
48	/VY/[1] A chain slipping out.
49	Vakulenchuk's head.
50	Hands.
51	Feet.
52	The funeral ribbon.
53	/ZHE/ Women's faces, singing. Diagonally from left, upwards.
54	A bollard and cable. Diagonally from right, downwards.
55	Prow of a ship. The anchor is hoisted.
56	The chain tightening.
57	Prow of a ship.
58	/RTV/ Prow of a ship.

---

[1] The words and parts of words distributed between frames 48 and 99 together compose a phrase from a revolutionary funeral march: *Vy zhe-rtv-oyu pa-li v bor'bye ro-ko-voi* — "you fell a victim in the fateful struggle". The title was evidently intended as the written equivalent of the "visual music" structuring this sequence. (For Eisenstein on the "visual music" of silent cinema, see his essay in *Film Form*.) However, in the course of montage, the rhythm and meaning of this "funeral symphony" — an arrangement of quick images of human grief rising to anger interplaying with shots of nature (the prow of the ship, the sea, buoys, silhouettes of sails, etc.) was felt to have been fully realised without written support, and the title was therefore dropped. (Transl.)

59	CU	The silt-covered anchor slipping out.
60		Shot of the same, from the other side.
61		Anchor buoy and chain.
62		/OYU/ Men's faces, singing. Diagonally from right, upwards.
63		A whaleboat is lowered to the water.
64	CU	Vakulenchuk.
65		A handkerchief raised to a face.
66		A hand dropping a copper coin.
67		Hands crumpling a cap.
68		Oars dipping towards the water.
69		[Rower's] arm movement (beginning of stroke).
70		Oars hitting the water.
71		[Rower's] head bending forward.
72		Fast double exposure /PA/.
73		Rower's heave on oars.
74		[His] mouth opening.
75		Fast double exposure, spurt straight at camera.[1]
76		Cranes.
77		The same.
78		Winch turning slowly.
79		A crumpled sail.
80		Pointed sail slipping up a mast.
81		Fast dissolve /LI/.
82		Wheels and pulleys moving.
83		Reflection of rising sail.
84		Crane descending.
85		The same.
86		Signal flags.
87		Peasant women prostrating themselves in grief.
88	CU	One of them raises her head.
89		A woman speaker (medium close shot) delivers a fiery speech.
90	MS	[The same woman] standing on a cask, other speakers in the background.
91		/V BOR'BYE/.

---

[1] The movement intended here seems to be that of the boat, rather than the rower, propelled forward by the oar stroke. (Transl.)

92		Fists.
93		A face, teeth clenched.
94		/RO/.
95		Beginning of oar stroke.
96		Oar striking the water.
97		/KO/.
98		Heave on oars.
99		/VOI/.
100		The whaleboat spurts forward.
101	CU	The woman speaker.
102	CU	Agitation among the crowd, speakers in the background.
103	CU	A worker.
104	CU	Fists.
105		Face, teeth clenched.
106		A man rips open his shirt.
107	CU	(Quick shot of) an old woman wiping away tears.
108	MS	A forest of fists.
109	CU	Face of the old woman ablaze . . .
110		Glotov, medium close shot.
111		The woman " Bundist "[1] speaking.
112	CU	Glotov's face, speaking.
113		DOWN WITH THE JEWS.
114		Insolent smirk on Glotov's face.
115⎫		
116⎬		Heads turn.
117⎭		
118		Glotov.
119		Shot of raised fists.
120		A speaker.
121		Glotov draws in his head.
122		Glotov, back to camera. The fists descend on him.
123		Glotov's face dissolves.
124	CU	Fists strike Glotov about the head.
125⎱		The whaleboat carves into the shore.
126⎰		

---

[1] The " Bund " — a Jewish socialist labour organisation which originated in the west of Russia in 1897. The woman is the one from frames 89, 90. (Transl.)

127		Speaker's head (Fel'dman)[1] in movement.
128	MS	Arrival of the whaleboat with sailors on board.
129		The crowd carrying the speaker.
130		A boathook moors the boat to the shore.
131		The men in the boat catch hold of the speaker.
132⟩	MS	Sailors hold a meeting on board the *Potemkin*.
133⟨		
134	LS	The meeting on board the battleship.
135		THE DELEGATE.
136	CU	The speaker (Fel'dman) comes into shot. He speaks [to the meeting].
137		General speech of welcome.

199[2]

The Red Flag is raised. Sloops sail up to the battleship with townspeople and provisions. *(Still)*

200

Sailors overturn a sloop carrying vodka.

---

[1] *Fel'dman,* Konstantin Isidorovich (1881-1968), was a member of the Russian Social-Democrat Workers' Party and was revolutionary Odessa's delegate on board the mutinous *Potemkin*. He appears as a speaker in the scene of the meeting on the mole.

[2] 199 (and 200 following). The frame numbering here apparently derives from the initial version of the script, a full text of which has not survived. In the original of the version published here, "The sailors overturn a sloop carrying vodka" is followed by the words "Steps, Nos 1-106" which have been deleted; it can be assumed from this that the elaboration of the frames in question dates from the period of work on the "Odessa Steps" sequence; and that in any case it pre-dates the recording of the remaining scripted scenes published here. Eisenstein was looking for the appropriate point in the narrative at which to introduce the episode of the meeting between the townspeople and the sailors of the *Potemkin*. That episode, elaborated in a few frames only, was originally placed at the end of the first section of the script: "196. Speech by the young student-orator (Fel'dman). 197. The crowd sends him as a delegate to the battleship. 198. Fel'dman on the *Potemkin* delivering a speech. 199. Raising the Red Flag. A vast crowd of boats sail up. They bring provisions, gifts, etc. 200. The sailors overturn the boat containing vodka. 201. Meeting on the *Potemkin*. Fel'dman speaks. 202. Theme of the title (A landing must be made)."
Eisenstein subsequently crossed out these frames, since the detailed elaboration of the funeral meeting which had become the second section of the script "shifted" them from this point in the narrative. Frames

1	LS	Iris in. The steps. People looking out [to sea]. *(Still)*
2	MS	People looking out.
3		Medium-close shot of people looking out, back to camera.
4		Two workers looking out.
5		A lady.
6		A cripple.
7		People point things out to children.
8		An elderly man mops his face. An old woman.
9		Girl students wave.
10		Two women.
11		Children are lifted into frame.
12		Old man watching.
13	CU	A child shouting.
14		The cripple moving among the legs of the crowd.
15		Medium close-shot of people reeling back.
15a		*The cripple closer.*
16		Legs collapsing.
17		The crowd rushing down.
18		Shot of legs, as people fall to their knees.
19		People rushing to the barrier (camera position outside).
20		A man falls into frame.
21		Legs of soldiers. *(Still)*
22		Shot from above of volley, backs [of soldiers] to camera.
23		People running down steps, away from camera.
24	LS	Panic on the steps.
25	MS	Flowers. Panic on the steps *(through the flower baskets).*
26		A group gathers at the wall.
27		People running through the flowers *(taken through lyre[1]).*

199-202 reappeared once again at the beginning of the final section (The End) — however, they were also excluded from here. In the final stages of work on the composition of the script, frames 199-200 found their place at the end of the second section — directly preceding the " Odessa Steps " sequence. In the course of shooting and montage processes, the content of these frames developed into the well-known episode involving " the sloops ".

[1] Part of the flower display. (Transl.)

28		Striding feet [of the soldiers].
29		People kneeling.
30		Flowers falling. *(Baskets.)*
31		Volley.
32		People falling into flowers. *(A basket topples . . .)*
32a		*The handle of a parasol snaps. The lace parasol covers the lens.*[1]
33		People jump over into the vine leaves.
33a		*The same.*
34		Falling into the flowers.
35		Striding feet.
36		Volley.
37	CU	People falling with the vine leaves.
37a		*The same in mid-shot.*
38		Legs running aside. A mother and children, advancing into camera.
39		Travelling shot down slope of steps, with mother and two children.
40		Volley.
41		The boy falls.
42	CU	The boy screaming.
43		The mother turns and screams.
44		Feet running over the boy.
44a		*The mother (closer than in 43).*
45		People dash to the wall. Children get tangled in the legs of the crowd.
46		Heads of panic-stricken old people.
46a	CU	*Vargach.*[2]
46b	CU	*' Pobedonostsev '.*[3]
46c	CU	*An elderly Jew.*
47		Striding feet.
48		Volley.
49		The group near the wall fall to the ground.

---

[1] What seems to be involved here is the " masking " of the frame by the movement of objects within it, i.e. their movement gives rise to a partial blocking of the field of vision.

[2] A member of the cast. (Transl.)

[3] *"Pobedonostsev":* this direction is concerned with " typage " — the need for a " type " evoking the Tsar's minister Pobedonostsev.

50		Mother rises into frame.
51		People pour past.
52		The mother mounts the steps. In the background soldiers descend, firing.
53	MS	The mother carries the slaughtered child (towards camera). *(Still)*
54		The mother's frantic appeal.
55		Poltavtseva rises out of a group of wounded.
56	CU	Poltavtseva.
57		The mother walks towards camera.
58		Poltavtseva's group moves forward.
59		Striding feet.
60		Volley.
61		The mother falls.
62		(The mother's fall).
63		The group around Poltavtseva falls.
63a		*People running (blurred effect). A young mother with pram is visible.*
63b		*The mother shields the pram, people run past her.*
63c		*The child in the pram, with mother's back in frame.*
64		Children run towards a " test-your-strength " machine.[1]
65		The children hide behind a tall man standing alongside the machine.
66		People's legs and children.
67		Volley.
68		Poltavtseva — dishevelled and screaming.
68a		*The mother gasps.*
68b		*Her hands clutch at her stomach.*
68c		*Her body sinks down in the frame.*
68d		*The front wheels of the pram on the edge of a step.*
68e		*The mother, back to camera, and the wheels of the pram. The end of the mother's fall (to a sitting position). The wheels jerk.*
68f		*The front wheels slip over the edge.*

---

[1] These were part of the Odessa steps location. Eisenstein incorporated the test-your-strength machine into a particular sequence (see frames 74-85) which was omitted at the montage stage because it slowed down the rhythm of the " Odessa Steps " sequence as a whole (Transl.)

68g		*The mother falls (onto back). The wheels leave the frame.*
68h	CU	*The pram starts rolling.*
68i		*From below, the steps and the pram starting to roll.*
68k		*A stout man near the dial [of the test-your-strength machine] shouts something, looking upwards.*
68l		*The mother turns on the ground.*
68m	CU	*Her face.*
68n		*From above, the pram bouncing down the steps.*
68o		*The tall man.*
69		The tall man *tries to move, but he is wounded,* [he] falls into the heap (of children) near the machine.
70		Volley.
71		Children near the easy chair,[1] screaming.
71a		*The pram moving slowly down.*
71b		*The mother drops back (she had half-raised herself).*
72		She tries to get up off the ground.
73		
74		A hand grabs the handle (of the test-your-strength machine).
75		A body straining.
76		**The needle [on the dial of the machine].**
76a		*(Travelling shot) the pram moving (from above).*
76b	CU	*(Travelling shot) the baby crying.*
77		Volley.
77a		*A mirror is shattered.*
77b		*The fragments fall over the stout man, who is rising to his feet.*
78		The tall man rises (beside)[2] the test-your-strength machine. *(Back to camera, reflected in the pieces of broken mirror).*
79		Volley.
80		The needle on the dial swings back.
81		The hand releases the handle.
81a		*Travelling shot of pram moving. (Wheels.)*
82		*The needle returns to its place.*

---

[1] " Children screaming " has been crossed out.
[2] " from behind " is crossed out here.

83		A body falls *(behind the machine)*.
84		Children falling.
84a		*The pram's front wheels strike the body.*
84b		*A wheel swivels.*
84c		*The pram comes to a halt on its front wheels (movement across the frame).*
84d		*The pram standing.*
85		The needle flickering.
86		Striding feet.
87		Volley.
87a	CU	of pram and child.
88		Striding feet *(with bodies in the foreground)*.
89		Volley.
89a		*Striding feet (over bodies).*
89b	CU	*[Soldiers'] boots and the mother.*
89c		*Volley.*
89d		*The pram, legs visible in the distance.*
89e		*Striding feet (bodies in the background).*
90		Bodies roll towards the bottom of the steps.
90a		*The pram.*
91		/Bodies roll towards the bottom of the steps./
91a		*[Soldiers'] legs in close-up advancing into camera.*
91b		*Volley.*
92		Poltavtseva's face, bloodied. *(Still)*
92a		*The pram.*
92b		*Poltavtseva with shattered pince-nez. The shutter closes vertically.*
93		The battleship opens fire.
		N.B. [for earlier] (a) Volley at the pram. The pram overturning (from behind). (b) Pram upside down. Bullet holes. Twisted axle.
93a		*Cupids.*[1]
93b		*The chariot (with panthers).*
94		Burst of shell fire [from the battleship], shallow focus.

---

[1] The original typescript contains a handwritten marginal note by Eisenstein, "on the theatre". This relates to frames 93a, 93b, 94a, 95, 96a, indicating that these frames refer to the sculptured ornaments on the Odessa Opera House.

94a		*Stone panthers (in close-up).*
95		The explosion *(at entrance gate* [to Odessa Opera House]).
95a		*The figure on the chariot.*
96	CU	Shell burst.
96a		*Masked cupids.*
97	CU	The blast (*iron grating* [Opera House gates]).
97a⎫ 97b⎭		*As above.*
98		Cossacks on the move.
99		The army (on the move).
100		Shell burst.
101		Blast.
102		A chimney topples.
103		/A chimney topples/.
104	CU	Shell burst.
105			The *Potemkin*'s angry response	
106		The sailors *holding a meeting* on the battleship.
107			on the atrocities in Odessa	
108		The meeting.
109		Fel'dman.
110			*on the need to make a landing*	
111[1]		
112[2]		

THE END

199–202[3]		
203 (1)		Sailors raise objections.
204 (2)		(Theme of sub-title: WE WILL AWAIT THE ARRIVAL OF THE SQUADRON — THEN WE WILL DECIDE.)
3	LS	The meeting on the deck.

---

[1] " Dissatisfied (sailors) " has been crossed out here.
[2] " A sailor " has been crossed out.
[3] After frames 199-202 the following has been crossed out: " Raising the Red Flag. A huge crowd of sloops sails up. They carry provisions, gifts, etc. A sloop carrying vodka is tipped into the sea by the sailors. Meeting on board the *Potemkin*. Fel'dman speaks. Theme of title (A LANDING HAS TO BE MADE)."

31

4		Dissolve to empty deck.
5		The sleeping battleship. Observation posts.[1]
1		Posts. (The watch? — find out). (Early morning.)
2		The look-out.
3		The committee. Three men asleep on sofas and floor. Two seated. A sailor comes in and says something.
4		The watch.
5		Sailors asleep beside their weapons.
6		[And] next to the shells.
7		[And] in the gun turret.
8		The sailor (on watch) walks past sleeping sailors.
9	LS	The sleeping battleship. Two sailors walk by.
10[2]		
11		A sleeping sailor.
12		The sleeping committee.
13		The watch. Two sailors walk by checking.
14		A sailor sleeping near the ship's gun jumps up, then reassured, goes back to sleep.
15		Two men in the gun turret raise their heads and then go back to sleep.
16 17 18		The sleeping battleship.
19		The look-out peers [into the distance].
20		The horizon. Smoke from the squadron's ships.
21		The look-out gives a signal.
22 23 24		Men wake up and run to look.
24a		The committee are informed. They start to run out.
25 26 27		The men look out, scrambling onto every possible vantage point.
28		The committee runs up on deck.
29		Everybody looks out.

---

[1] "To be shot from the foot of the *Potemkin* rear mast" is crossed out.

[2] The content of this frame is missing from the original.

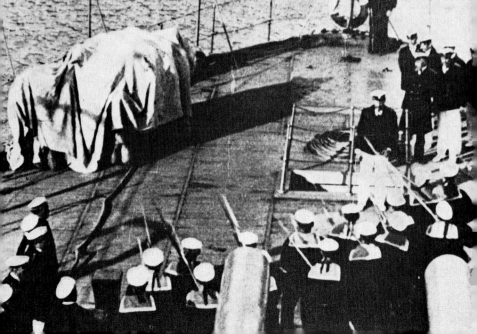

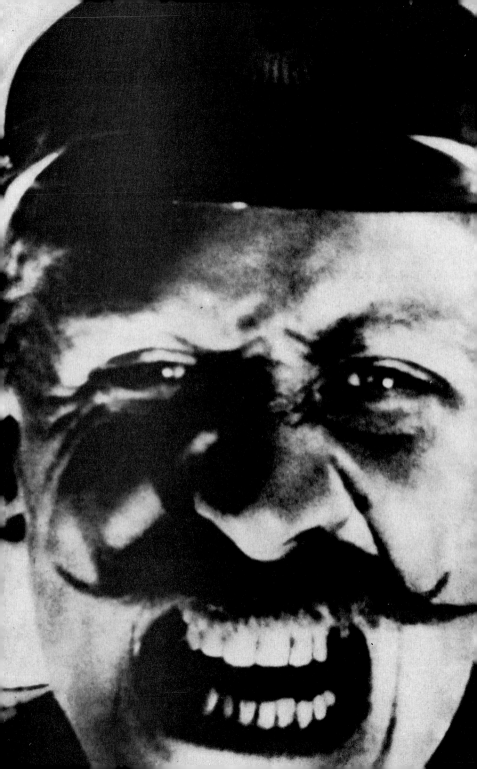

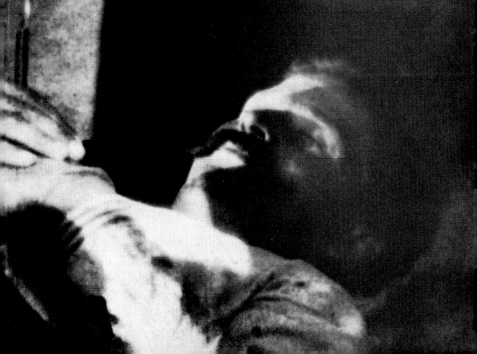

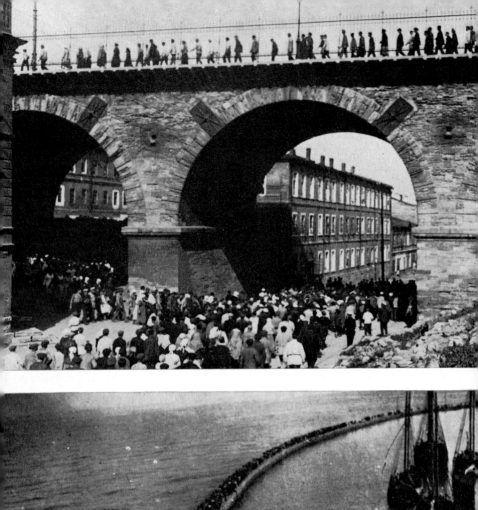

30	A command is given. (Action stations.)
31	
32	
33	
34	Action stations. (Preparations.)
35	
36	
37	
38	The committee looks through telescope.
39	The squadron has drawn closer.
40	Action stations. (Preparations.)
41	
42	The deck is hosed down.
42a	Men hosing the decks.
42b	
43	Guns turning.
44	From the handrail [of the battleship]. Other guns turning.
45	The deck. Flowing water. Water and legs running into frame.
46	In the foreground a sailor hoses down the decks. Others in the background.
47	Sailor looks to the left.
48	Gun turret and guns swing (camera position on the battleship).
49	Sailor looks to the right.
50	Gun turret and guns swing.
51	Medium close shot of the sailor with a jet of water. Laughing. He swings the jet to the right.
52	GUNS TO THE RIGHT.
53	He laughs.
54	Hands swinging the jet of water to the left.
55	The sailor's face.
56	GUNS TO THE LEFT.
57	Medium close shot of the sailor swinging the jet of water back.
58	
59	The sailors break off their " duties " and turn their heads. One of them laughs.
60	

61	MS	The deck. A sailor dances around hosing down the deck, swinging the jet of water from right to left.
62		The look-out shouts something.
63		THE SQUADRON HAS SAILED PAST.
63a		*The muzzle of a gun rises into frame.*
64		The sailor lowers the jet.
65		Everyone is laughing and looking out [into the distance].
66		The departing squadron.
67	CU	The bugler, sounding a call. Dissolve.
68 69 70		Dissolve. The sailors munching food. The look-out.
71		The squadron turns around.
72		The look-out gives a signal.
73		Everyone raises his head.
74		The signal.
75		A cauldron of soup is knocked over.
76 77 78		Legs running up ladders.
79 80		Shells sliding over cables.
81		An order is given over the speaking tube.
82		The anchor is lifted from the water.
83		The squadron draws nearer.
84 85		In the *Potemkin*'s engine room.
86		The men loading shells.
87		General view of guns at the ready.
88		The squadron draws nearer.
89		The committee on the watch tower.
90 91 92		The empty deck.
93 94		The sailors standing motionless by the guns.
95		Nearer shot of squadron approaching.
96		Massive guns.
97	LS	The squadron's guns swing in.

98	The sailors embrace [farewell?]. One sailor is about to fire, another restrains him.
100	Massive guns pointed at camera.
101	A sailor dashes away from his post.
102	The squadron draws nearer.
103	Guns swing towards camera.
104	Aerial shot. The *Potemkin* sails into the squadron.
105	From one side ⟩ The *Potemkin* entering [the squadron].
106	From the other ⟨
107	Sailors standing on the decks of the ships.
108	The *Potemkin* carves its way in. (From the mast of the *Potemkin*.)
109	The side of the *Potemkin* as it sails past the *Sinop*. The sailors standing on the deck of the *Sinop* cheer.
110	On board the *Rostislav*, the crew run out on deck. They cheer.
111	On the topmost parts of the *Potemkin*, men cheering and throwing their caps in the air. *(Still)*
112	On the deck of the *Potemkin*, men cheering and throwing their caps in the air.
113	The *Potemkin*, from behind, as it sails out of the corridor. A general cheering — from the whole squadron. Everyone is throwing his cap in the air.
114	The *Potemkin* sails full speed to the camera. Caps fly into the air and into the water.
115	The prow of the *Potemkin* — towards camera. Waves.

The international career of *Battleship Potemkin* and its wide-ranging effect on world film production began with its enthusiastic reception in Berlin. It is impossible now to comprehend that *Potemkin*, which announced to the world that there was a Soviet cinema, might not have reached that world outside the Soviet Union had it not been for the loud persuasion of Vladimir Mayakovsky, one of the few Russian intellectuals to realize at once its extraordinary worth.

In spite of the German censors — or perhaps because of their intense concern with this unclassifiable film — Berlin workers and intellectuals so filled the small cinema where it was first shown that the Soviet film office in Berlin withdrew the film, to remove the "objectionable" scenes, to improve it a little (for the rest of its commercial life people were always "improving" *Potemkin*) and prepare for a re-opening in a larger theatre. They also commissioned Edmund Meisel, a young musician in the Piscator-Brecht circle, to compose a score for its new presentation, and invited Eisenstein to come and meet the dazzled press and puzzled film-people of Berlin. The spirited arrogance of the twenty-eight-year-old film-maker exactly fitted their image of *Potemkin*'s creator. They were not so prepared for his polished, witty use of the German language, and his brief stay was a social success. There was talk of him working in the well-equipped film studios of Berlin, but only talk. He returned to Moscow to continue the preparation of the film on agriculture that he had been assigned, and *Potemkin* went on to lasting international fame.

OCTOBER

Halfway through the filming of their agricultural policy film (begun as *The General Line*) the Eisenstein group — Alexandrov and Tisse completed the triumvirate — were given another, quite different and quite urgent film assignment. *Gen-Line* was reluctantly left hanging, unresolved, and the group began work on *October,* one of the several films planned for the tenth anniversary of the Revolution, meaning the Bolshevik Revolution of October, 1917.

In assigning *October* to the Eisenstein group the committee making the decision was sure of one thing, they wanted "another *Potemkin*! " That the people who had reconstructed the Odessa of 1905 had changed and grown (with incredible speed) was a vital fact of no interest to the committee, and most of *October*'s difficulties stemmed from that blindness. The concentration in a limited time-space of the earlier film was reflected in the first title announced for the new project, "Ten Days That Shook the World", a title John Reed's account had made worldfamiliar.* But the first idea for the Eisenstein-Alexandrov scenario, dated November 7, 1926, covered far too much time to be described as "Ten Days". It extended from the overthrow of the monarchy in the February Revolution to the end of the Civil War. Early in 1927 (the year of production and celebration had already begun!) there was an agreement to divide the monster scenario (echoes of *The Year 1905*) into two parts — first filming Part One, from the February to the October Revolutions, and then, if there was time (!), or "later," Part Two, the Civil War.†

On February 5 the draft of Part One was accepted by the committee,‡ and the rest of the month Eisenstein and Alexandrov worked on the shooting script. This too was submitted (not without argument — for this was not the *Potemkin* nor the simple reconstruction of the events of 1917 that the committee expected), and was revised throughout March. When the group started filming in mid-April (the scene of fraternisation, see p. 52), the arguments were by no means finished, but *October* was begun.

---

* Eisenstein's teacher, Meyerhold, had announced in 1925 that he intended to film Reed's chronicle.

† The whole of this unrealized Part Two of *October* is translated, below, in the appendix. Two earlier projects were incorporated into Part Two: Eisenstein's adaptation of Serafimovich's *Iron Flood,* and a glimpse of *Perekop.*

‡ "Even the preliminary sketches for the scenario required far more time than had been allocated to this stage of the work." Eisenstein, in *Kino Gazeta,* December 20, 1927.

OCTOBER

In collaboration with Grigori Alexandrov

Despite the frame numbering, the term " shooting script " is not a strictly accurate description of the following script. It is, however, the latest version (dating from late 1926 and early 1927) and the one which most closely resembles the film. Since the film had to be completed for the Tenth Anniversary of the Revolution, Eisenstein had scarcely six months to complete *October,* and a full version of the shooting script never in fact existed — scenes were constantly re-worked during shooting. Eisenstein originally conceived of the film on an epic scale, to take in the February and October revolutions, and with a sequel on the Civil War. Extracts from these versions appear in the appendix.

*   *   *

Act One

1   Gold,
2   precious stones,
3   shimmering lights covered the tsarist crown, the imperial sceptre and the autocratic orb.
4   The gold glittered,
5   the lights shone,
6   the gems sparkled,
7   until . . . until women's bony fists rose out of the queues of the hungry.
8   until calloused workers' hands brought machines to a standstill,
9   until angry leaflets lifted into the air,
10   until the hungry trenches ceased firing,
11   until the people rose up and brandished their fists.
12   But see, they have risen,
13   and they have brandished their fists,
14   And with that the crown began to grow tarnished and dull,
15   with that, the blinding radiance faded,
16   with that, the oppressive, crushing idol became visible . . .

17   The idol of autocracy, standing

18   on a massive, polished stone, against a sky darkened by ominous clouds.

19   Colossal demonstrations seethed like the waves of the ocean.

20   Wave after wave of the workers' masses,

21   wave after wave of the mass of peasants and soldiers,

22   wave after wave they flowed in to swell the ninth wave . . .

23   And on the crest of this general surge of exultation, a small, living, working man set his foot on the huge imperial crown,

24   on the cast-iron crown of the statue of Alexander III.

25   A monument which stood in the shelter of the golden cupolas of " Christ the Saviour " near tramway line A.

26   Living hands placed a — fatal — noose around the metallic imperial neck.

27   The rope was drawn.

28   The noose tightened . . .

29   The clamps burst . . .

30   Swaying, the doll toppled from its tall pedestal,

31   and fell to the ground, shattering into fragments.

32   And words flew up like spray —

TO ALL! TO ALL! TO ALL!

33   To the prisons with their pale prisoners,

34   To the towns, the steppes, the fields.

35   To the Georgians, the Kirghiz, the Finns.

TO ALL! TO ALL!

36   And to the bourgeois and intellectuals assembled in the Tauride Palace.[1]

TO ALL!

37   To the generals.

38   To the merchants.

39   To the police.

LONG MAY THEY LIVE!

40   The archdeacons contorted their mouths to howl:

---

[1] Seat of the Duma, established in 1906 following on the 1905 uprising. (Transl.)

LONG LIVE THE PROVISIONAL GOVERNMENT!

41 The Metropolitan of Novgorod hailed the government with public prayer...

42 A provincial commissioner of police welcomed Rodzianko with a telegram:

> " AS A SECRET REPUBLICAN OF SEVENTEEN YEARS' STANDING, I HAVE THE HONOUR TO CONGRATU-LATE YOUR EXCELLENCY..."

43 Bells pealed...

44 Censers smoked...

45 The orators of the petty-bourgeois party poured forth like balalaikas.

46 The telegraph machines tapped away like trilling nightingales.

TO ALL... TO ALL... TO ALL...

47 But, like ammonia hitting the nostrils, a question sprang to the eye:

T-O A-L-L?

48 What of those at the front, ragged, famished and deathly pale,
49 standing barefoot in cold pools of blood,
50 their skins pierced by red-hot splinters?

T-O A-L-L? T-O A-L-L?

51 What of the peasant women without men?
52 And the old people of the village with no one to relieve them?
53 And the children left without fathers?
54 And the hungry peasants without horses?

T-O A-L-L? T-O A-L-L? T-O A-L-L?

55 And the workers whose wives stand in hungry queues as before,
56 whose hands shape shells in the factories as before?

T-O A-L-L?

57 The front. If that's the case, then it's down bayonets!
58 To hell with officers! *(Scene of soldiers defying an officer.)*

59 A kiss for whiskery lips.
60 A hug from powerful paws.
61 Brother . . .
62 Brother.

FRATERNISATION.

63 The iron helmet on Ivan.
64 The fur cap on Hans.
65 Hands joined in heartfelt handshake.

BUT . . .

66 A figure whose thinness was due to breeding not hunger stood bowing obsequiously on the gleaming parquet floor of an allied embassy.
67 The figure held out a paper clenched between manicured fingernails.
68 A paper known as a " note ".

THE PROVISIONAL GOVERNMENT . . . WILL RESPECT ITS OBLIGATIONS TOWARDS OUR ALLIES IN THEIR ENTIRETY.

69 The officers swore oaths, hands on swords.
70 A special burst of shrapnel drove the fraternising soldiers back into the trenches.
71 The Central Committee of the Menshevik Party maintained a treacherous silence. (Meeting of the Central Committee: to consider the Provisional Government's note.)
72 Soldiers, into the trenches! Soldiers, into battle!
73 If not, bullets in your heels.
74 If not, bullets in your back.

T-O A-L-L?

75 If that's so, let's take the landowners' lands,
76 share out the ploughs, the grain, the livestock.
77 But again . . .

BUT . . .

78 Cracking the whip,
79 the Provisional Government urged:

WAIT!
WAIT!
WAIT FOR THE CONSTITUENT ASSEMBLY!

80 The commissars of the Provisional Government used the Cossacks, whose name means " force, arbitrary rule " in every language of the world,

81 used them to drive the peasants from the land, the livestock and the machines,

82 used them to drive the newly-awakened peasantry back into darkness, into unrelieved night.

83 Into that darkness,

84 that unrelieved night,

85 broke a sudden ray of light.

86 A floodlight beam — first one, then two, then three.

87 Those arrows of light swung from end to end illuminating a sea of heads

88 at the Finland Station.

89 Illuminating the faces of seven thousand workers and soldiers who had turned towards the light.

90 Illuminating the flags of the Petrograd Committee, and the young soldiers watching the figure of the " old soldier of the Revolution " rise before them on an armoured car:

UL'YANOV
LENIN. (Still)

91 Ilyich waited a long time for the storm of enthusiasm to die down, then he raised his hand.

92 Everyone fell silent — stillness reigned.

NO SUPPORT
FOR THE PROVISIONAL GOVERNMENT!

93 Concentration showed on the faces of the crowd.

LONG LIVE THE SOCIALIST REVOLUTION!
S-O-C-I-A-L-I-S-T!
A REPUBLIC OF SOVIETS OF WORKERS AND PEA-SANTS' DEPUTIES THROUGH THE ENTIRE LAND, FROM TOP TO BOTTOM.

94 A still sea of faces.

LONG LIVE THE SOCIALIST REVOLUTION!
S-O-C-I-A-L-I-S-T!

95 Pulling up his collar and drawing his head back into his shoulders, a morose man climbed into a car.

THE PRESIDENT OF THE PETROGRAD SOVIET
CHKHEIDZE.[1]

while the word

SOCIALIST

96 was already on its way to the Duma,
97 to the Winter Palace,
98 to Petrograd,
99 to the whole vast land of Russia.

SOCIALIST.

Act Two

SOCIALISTS, NOT BOURGEOIS.
DOWN!
DOWN WITH THE PROVISIONAL GOVERNMENT!

100 Sailors from Kronstadt,
101 factory workers
103 and women workers from the mills and factories filled the avenues, streets and lanes to overflowing.
104 Songs, bands, slogans.
105 A boiling, bubbling human cauldron.
106 The " Marseillaise " and the " Warsovienne ".
107 Flags and placards.
108 Slogans and shouts — everything flowed into one in the echoing streets of Petrograd.
109 But one note . . .
110 one slogan . . .
111 one forceful idea broke to the surface.
112 It broke to the surface and took the lead.
113 Idea. Slogan. Poster.

---

[1] The Menshevik Nikolai Chkheidze (1865-1926). (Transl.)

114 As the drowning man clutches at a straw, so the failing government reaches for the machine gun.

115 Government machine guns sprayed the " rioters " with lead on the corner of Sadovaya Street and Nevsky Prospect.

116 The window panes of quiet apartments rang out as they shattered, people screamed as they ran into doorways and alleys.

117 Blood flowed on the asphalt, mingling with the dust and the husks of sunflower seeds.

118 July 3-5. Famous days. Days when the demands of the proletariat broke to the surface.

119 Days when the mass of people could not hold back their fury.

JULY 3-5

120 Memorable days when the bourgeoisie and social-traitors gave free reign to their itches.

121 Their itch to get at the bolsheviks.

122 The offspring of the bourgeoisie, turned brutal, beat up workers in the streets. *(Stills)*[1]

123 They raided Kshesinskaya's Palace[2] where a plate hung over the door

CENTRAL COMMITTEE OF THE WORKERS' SOCIAL-DEMOCRAT PARTY OF RUSSIA (BOLSHEVIK).

124 They smeared that plate and trampled it under foot.

125 They caught sight of the worker Voinov carrying a copy of " *The Soldiers' Pravda* " and converged on him, punching his face, tearing at him and breaking his arms and legs.

126 In " The Crosses "[3] a far-sighted government made ready a prison cell.

127 The floors of the cell were washed.

128 The lock checked.

129 The bars tested.

---

[1] Stills 2 and 3 show scenes of workers attacked by women with parasols which, though appearing in the film, are not specifically mentioned in this script.

[2] The sumptuous house of Kshesinskaya, prima ballerina and former mistress of the Tsar, became the headquarters of the Bolshevik Party.

[3] One of the prisons in the Petropavlovskaya Fortress.

FOR UL'YANOV LENIN.

130   Taken in by lies, cyclists tore up " *The Soldiers' Pravda* " and
       the shreds scattered over the streets, floated like
131   feathers in a Jewish pogrom. This was called
       LIBERAL DEMOCRACY MENSHEVIC-STYLE.
132   The prisons and casements were crowded with the maimed.

DICTATOR
SUPREME COMMANDER
AND SO FORTH . . . AND SO FORTH . . .
KERENSKY

133   shook hands with the palace footmen as he divested himself
       of his coat in the hall. *(Still)*[1]
134   In the prisons, the

" TRAITORS "

135   to us — sailors of Kronstadt.
136   In the casemates, the

" BETRAYERS "

137   to us — factory workers.

BOLSHEVIKS

138   to us — the party driven underground
139   to us — Lenin, in hiding in a hut.
140   There were peasants too in the prisons.
141   Imprisoned by

THE SOCIALIST-MINISTER AVKSENT'EV.

142   A minister who, even when he hailed a cabby, did so in the
       name of one hundred million peasants. He nevertheless con-
       signed peasants to prison

FOR HAVING SHARED OUT THE LAND WITHOUT
AUTHORISATION.

143   A riding-crop, hat and gloves casually thrown on the sump-

---

[1] Still shows Kerensky's ascent of the Winter Palace staircase, which
immediately precedes this point in the film.

tuous imperial bed in the Winter Palace.
144 Braces hanging from the crystal chandelier.
145 A sportsman's gaiters dangling from a gilt easy chair.

ALEXANDER FYODOROVICH . . . IN THE APART-
MENTS OF ALEXANDRA FYODOROVNA.

146 Wearing a dressing gown and his habitual ironic smile, he is
signing an order

FOR THE RE-INSTITUTION OF CAPITAL PUNISH-
MENT.

147 He inserts the final full stop and rises proudly " to view all
the world as muck, himself as Bonaparte ". It's ludicrous.
148 But for some reason the sirens are hooting in the Petrograd
factories.
149 For some reason the sirens are wailing in the suburbs.
150 Their wailing is not heard in the Winter Palace.
151 Kerensky is busy changing the monogram on the imperial bed,
152 where, under the letter " A ", there stands a Roman three.
153 And so under that " A ", his fingers are transforming the three
into a Roman four. Which gives him " Alexander IV ". It's
diverting.
154 But for some reason the sirens carry on hooting.
155 For some reason groups of workers are hurrying into the
suburbs.
156 For some reason people are erupting on every corner as from
some human explosion.

FRUITS OF THE RE-ESTABLISHMENT OF DISCIPLINE.

157 With British tanks,
158 French aeroplanes,
159 with armoured trains and the " wild division ",

GENERAL KORNILOV

advances on revolutionary Petrograd.
160 There is little hope of good to be seen in the faces of the
" wild division ".
161 There is little hope of good to be read in the General's order:

57

WITH BLOOD AND IRON,
IN THE NAME OF GOD AND COUNTRY . . .
DESTROY THE AGENTS OF THE GERMAN GENERAL
STAFF (THE BOLSHEVIKS).

162   Tanks, armoured trains, batteries.
163   Kerensky lets his head sink onto the table.

THE GOVERNMENT IS POWERLESS.

164   The sirens go on hooting. From the suburbs, factories and plants, ever new reinforcements come

TO THE DEFENCE OF PETROGRAD.

165   The Red Guards grab rifles.
166   The Red Guards move swiftly towards the town gates.
167   The Red Guards assemble and receive orders in the courtyard of the Smolny Institute.
168   Lights beaming from the windows of the Smolny break up the foggy night.
169   The fiery speeches of its orators galvanise the energies of the departing troops.
170   Its ceaseless " shower " of pamphlets organises the aspirations of the masses.
171   All the surviving Bolsheviks are given a commissar's mandate and take command of Red units.
172   Although pointsmen on the railways had sent Kornilov's trains to dead-ends.
173   and for the moment those special trains could go no further, the city was nevertheless held in a circle, a circle of hostile armies.
174   Orders from the Smolny " opened the prison gates ".
175   And the prisoners turned into revolutionary fighters on the spot.
176   As they dashed out of the prisons, workers and sailors grabbed rifles on the run.
177   They loaded them on the run.

" TRAITORS "

178   — Red Guards in an armoured vehicle, racing to the defence.

179 — a lorryload of sailors, bristling with bayonets.

BOLSHEVIKS

180 — " colourless " figures in workers' and soldiers' dress infiltrating the very heart of the " wild division ",
181 agitators, slipping under the buffers of the armoured train, sliding in among piles of timber,
182 representatives of the Smolny, bringing the men of the " wild division " — from Turkmenia and Dagestan — tracts in their own languages.
183 Tracts which revealed:

WHO IS BEHIND KORNILOV.

184 Slipping into the armoured train on that dark August night, these " inflammatory " men told the dragoons and artillery

FOR WHAT
AND FOR WHOM KORNILOV FIGHTS.

It was enough.
185 The soldiers of the " wild division " and the Bolsheviks from the Smolny

FRATERNISED.

186 The Georgians danced the *lezginka*.
187 The emissaries from the Petrograd Soviet danced the *trepak*.

BREAD! PEACE! LAND!
POWER TO THE WORKERS!

188 The Bolshevik Party programme was transformed into a weapon against infantry, cavalry and artillery.
189 On this occasion, iron, powder and steel proved powerless.

GENERAL KORNILOV WAS ARRESTED.

Act Three

THE COUNTER-REVOLUTION WAS SUPPRESSED, BUT
THE REVOLUTIONARY PROLETARIAT DID NOT LAY
DOWN THEIR ARMS.

190 In factory blocks, factories and on vacant lots, the workers' guard trained in the use of the bayonet and the rifle. *(Still)*
191 In all corners of the suburbs, instructors back from the front passed on their military skills to the workers.
192 . . . The hut stood on the territory of Razliv Station.
193 But its sphere of influence was much wider.

EITHER RENOUNCE THE SLOGAN
" ALL POWER TO THE SOVIETS "
OR REVOLT — THERE IS NO MIDDLE WAY.

194 This was the message of the letters from the hut.

WE MUST, MUST SEIZE POWER

195 ran like a crimson thread through these letters.

WE MUST

because
196 at a meeting in Kronstadt, the sailors voted

FOR THE SOVIET

197 because after Krylenko's fiery speech, the great arm of the struggle — the Petrograd armoured base — voted

FOR THE SOVIET

198 because, at immense meetings held in the Ciniselli and " Modern " circuses, thousands of arms, voting with colts and Nagans[1] were raised

FOR THE SOVIET

199 because five squadrons from five Russian seas were

FOR THE SOVIET.

200 While the newspapers of the time wrote of a " Bolshevik plot ".
201 They wrote of a plot when
202 126 telegrams
203 from 126 Soviets demanded

---

[1] A revolver used in the Russian Army; name derived from Belgian *Nagant*.

THE TRANSFER OF POWER.

204 They wrote of a plot when
205 the fires of insurrection had sparked off

80 PROVINCES.

206 The Smolny prepared for a Congress of Soviets.
207 Its preparations were as intensive as for a major campaign.
208 The outcome of the insurrection more or less depended on the armed soldiers.
209 In short, the outcome was in the hands of the Petrograd Garrison.
210 And this is where the Smolny directed most of its preparatory work.
211 The Government smelt a rat, and rapped out an order from the General Staff:

THE GARRISON MUST LEAVE THE CITY AT ONCE.

212 The Soviet of Workers' Deputies set up their own staff

THE MILITARY-REVOLUTIONARY COMMITTEE.

213 That committee sent its commissars into the General Staff to check on its activities.
214 Colonel Polkovnikov told the commissars:

THE GENERAL STAFF DOES NOT RECOGNISE THE POWERS OF THE SOVIET OF DOGS' DEPUTIES.

215 The Central Committee of the Bolshevik Party held a secret meeting in a private flat.

ON OCTOBER 10.

216 Lenin was present at that meeting.

IN VIEW OF EVENTS

the meeting placed

ARMED INSURRECTION

217 on the Order of the Day.
218 The Congress of Soviets was fixed for the 25th.

61

THE CONGRESS MUST BE CONFRONTED WITH THE
ACCOMPLISHED FACT.

The 24th would be too soon — the 26th too late.

219 The uprising is decided for the 25th.
220 The Petrograd garrison justified the hopes of the Petrograd
proletariat.
221 Justified them proudly by adopting the one resolution at all
its regimental meetings:

THE PETROGRAD GARRISON NO LONGER RECOG-
NISES THE PROVISIONAL GOVERNMENT.
WE SHALL OBEY ONLY THE ORDERS OF THE PETRO-
GRAD SOVIET, ISSUED BY ITS MILITARY-REVOLU-
TIONARY COMMITTEE.

222 Fifty-one military units accepted the commissars from Smolny
and carried out no order without their sanction.
223 Disarmed by the Government, the military units armed themselves by opening up the arsenals.
224 The outcome of the uprising also depended on a second force.
225 On the Petrograd proletariat.
226 The Military-Revolutionary committee exerted all its strength
to arm the proletariat.

ON ORDERS FROM SMOLNY THE SESTRORETSKY
FACTORY

227 issued 50,000 rifles.
228 Factory delegates were issued with rifles from arms depots and
gun shops, on orders from the Military-Revolutionary Committee.
229 The Smolny was transformed into an arsenal.
230 The Institute became a revolutionary camp.
231 An uninterrupted stream of people flowed in and out of its
doors.
232 The stream overflowed up and down its staircases and
corridors.
233 Armoured vehicles, cars, motorcycles, bicycles, units of the
Red Guard, issued with mandates and instructions, made their
way to appointed destinations.

234 The Red Guards rolled machine gun carriages *(Still and plan)* across the stone-floor corridors, and the metallic clatter of the wheels frightened people sitting behind doors marked

RUSSIAN SOCIAL-DEMOCRAT PARTY (MENSHEVIK).

235 In the upper rooms they loaded cartridges.
236 In the lower ones they cleaned the machine guns.
237 In room 10, three very different men pored over a map.
238 Chudnovsky.
239 Podvoisky.
240 Antonov-Ovseyenko.

THE MILITARY TROIKA OF THE MILITARY-REVOLU-TIONARY COMMITTEE.

241 The troika was elaborating a plan of campaign.
242 Fingers leapt from one city gate to the next across the map of Petrograd spread out on an iron bedstead.
243 They drew a circle around the Palace.

Act Four

THE EVE OF THE 25TH.

244 A cold, foggy night.
245 Lights shone from the Smolny's numerous windows.
246 Torches flickered near the entrance.
247 Fires glowed in the gardens.
248 Sentries grouped themselves around the fires. *(Still)*
249 One after another, units leave for the city.
250 One after another, orders fly along the telegraph wires from a small room.
251 One after another, regiments occupy the city gates.
252 One after another, units occupy:
253 the railway stations,
254 the power stations,
255 the water works.
256 Near the Franco-Russian factory, the training ship

AURORA

rocks on the waves of the Neva.

63

257 The cruiser is ready. Prepared for action.

258 The sailors are ready to go into action on the sea and in the streets.

259 Silence reigns over the fog-wrapped city.

260 Its inhabitants peacefully sleep.

261 The steady tramp of units of the Red Guard breaks the silence, heightening the growing tension.

> HELSINGFORS. CENTROBALT. SEND REGULATION.
> Y. SVERDLOV.[1]

262 Decoded this reads:

> SEND LANDING FORCE AND BATTLESHIPS.
> THE MILITARY-REVOLUTIONARY COMMITTEE.

263 The telegram arrives.

264 Silence in the dark streets of Helsingfors.

265 Silently, without sounding their foghorns, tugboats begin to approach the shore one by one.

266 Moored, they disembark companies of soldiers.

267 The companies climb into trains and convoy after convoy makes its way to Petrograd.

268 Dawn has not yet broken.

269 The fog has not quite lifted.

270 But already units occupy:

271 the telegraph office,

272 the telephone exchange,

273 the water works,

274 the power stations,

275 the railway stations.

276 One after another, units leave the Smolny in a steady stream.

277 One after another, orders flow along the electrified telegraph wires in a steady stream.

278 The minelayers carve their majestic way through the water in battle order.

279 They move soundlessly, their signal lights flickering.

280 The morning breeze lifts their flags which carry the Baltic fleet's programme of action in bold letters:

---

[1] Yakov Sverdlov (1885-1919), one of Lenin's closest collaborators.

ALL POWER TO THE SOVIETS.

281 The Provisional Government issued a command:

THE CRUISER AURORA WILL PUT TO SEA AT ONCE,

and with little hope of the order being carried out, they sent two armoured vehicles to back it up.

282 In the first place, gun turrets are not afraid of machine guns.

283 In the second place, printing machines had already published a call

TO THE CITIZENS OF RUSSIA:
THE PROVISIONAL GOVERNMENT HAS BEEN
DEPOSED
THE GOVERNMENT HAS PASSED TO THE ORGAN OF
THE SOVIET OF WORKERS' AND SOLDIERS'
DEPUTIES — TO THE MILITARY-REVOLUTIONARY
COMMITTEE, WHICH IS AT THE HEAD OF THE PRO-
LETARIAT AND THE GARRISON.

284 That's why the command simply made the *Aurora*'s crew laugh.

285 That's why the armoured vehicles turned around and put distance between themselves and the muzzles of her guns.

LONG LIVE THE WORKERS' AND PEASANTS'
REVOLUTION!
THE MILITARY-REVOLUTIONARY COMMITTEE OF
THE PETROGRAD WORKERS' AND SOLDIERS'
DEPUTIES.
OCTOBER 25, 1917, 10 A.M.

286 These were the concluding words of the proclamation — printed on leaflets which were brought in lorryloads to the Smolny.

ORDERS FROM THE MILITARY-REVOLUTIONARY
COMMITTEE

287 And the *Aurora* carried them out at once.

288 It drove the cadets from Nikolaevsky Bridge.

289 It landed units.

290 It lowered the raised bridge. (*Still*)

291 And mounted guard.

WHY ARE THE COSSACKS NOT HERE YET?

292 Kerensky demands agitatedly over the telephone.
293 [A Cossack] replies:

THEY'RE JUST SADDLING UP THE HORSES.

294 That's what he says, but the saddles are hanging on hooks in the stables.
295 The horses are quietly munching their hay and the Cossack groom is packing his pipe with tobacco.

WHY ARE THE ARMOURED VEHICLES NOT HERE YET?

296 Kerensky shouts down the receiver.
297 The base replies:

THEY'RE JUST FILLING UP WITH FUEL.

298 Kerensky jumps up, seeing a way out:

MAKE FOR THE FRONT AND, AT THE HEAD OF TROOPS LOYAL TO THE GOVERNMENT . . . CRUSH THEM . . .

299 A car fluttering an American flag pulls up at the entrance to General Headquarters.
300 Meanwhile the Cossack horses munch their hay and the Cossacks maintain their neutrality.
301 Accompanied by his elegant aides-de-camp, Kerensky climbs into the car. He is escorted by Kishkin, Pal'chinsky and Rutenberg.
302 Meanwhile the letters

R.S.D.R.P.[1]

are being chalked on the armoured vehicles over names like "Oleg", "Yaroslav".
303 The American car races through the streets and officers salute the Prime Minister as he passes.

450

---

[1] The initials of the Russian Social-Democrat (Bolshevik) Party.

304 Number after number is entered into books by the girls working with the committee checking credentials at the Second Congress of Soviets.

305 From Siberia . . .

306 From the front . . .

307 From the Ukraine . . .

308 From the front . . .

309 One after another the delegates fill the corridors and rooms of the Smolny.

310 Some fresh from prison.

311 Some fresh from the trenches.

312 Rough, simple faces, sailors' jackets, officers' epaulettes, the faces of intellectuals, move past in the spit-spattered corridors of the Smolny Institute.

313 Kerensky's car gathers speed.

314 Passing sailors stare in amazement at the car rushing furiously past them.

315 A constant stream of couriers runs out of the room of the Military-Revolutionary Committee.

316 One after another the units execute orders.

317 By now a cannon has been installed on the Politseisky Bridge.

318 By now streets have been blocked off by patrols of soldiers, sailors and workers.

319 The unanimous meeting at the Petropavlovskaya Fortress is over by now, and the soldiers have banked up guns on the fortress parapet.

320 The American car continues to pick up speed.

321 The latest delegate's credentials:

NO. 562 FROM KRONSTADT.

322 The rooms of the Smolny are crammed with people.

323 In one of the rooms lie piles of the proclamation which indicates

10 A.M.

324 while the tramway clock already shows long past midday.

325 Faster and faster run the couriers.

326   The telephones ring more and more frequently.

ON ITS WAY TO GATCHINA

327   the frantic car speeds through the Narvskaya gates.
328   The sentry doesn't have time to leap into the roadway.
329   In the Malachite room of the Palace

THE PROVISIONAL GOVERNMENT

is seated motionless at a round table.
330   The empty place of the Prime Minister shows like a broken tooth.
331   The officer cadets cross from Kirochnaya Square to the square in front of the Palace.
332   Inside the gates of the Winter Palace a woman officer issues a command to the women's shock battalion. *(Still)*
333   The Georgievsky élite regiment takes up positions on the ground floor.
334   The artillery unit erects its guns in the square.
335   The cadets from the engineering corps training school build a barricade along the Palace facade with piles of firewood.
336   This is at the Winter Palace.
337   But at the Smolny the large white hall is packed to overflowing.
338   People are perched in the galleries, on the base of pillars and on window ledges.
339   The room is crammed with people — there are more than 600 delegates.
340   The second hand ticks on and the impatience of the delegates grows.
341   The proclamation said " 10 a.m. ", but by now the tramway clocks show five minutes to eight in the evening.
342   The second hand ticks on.
343   In room 10, a pencil is drawing a line between crosses on the map of Petersburg.
344   The first cross — a unit of Red Guards waiting motionless under the triumphal arch.
345   The pencil draws a line from cross to cross.
346   The second cross — a soldiers' post at the Admiralty.
347   The third — the *Aurora* at Nikolaevsky Bridge, guns at the ready.

348 The fourth.
349 The fifth.
350 The sixth.
351 A tower on the People's House, manned by a unit of riflemen.
352 The fortress across the Neva, ready for action; a lorryful of
     sailors at the corner of an alleyway.
353 The pencil completes the circle at the first cross. It has closed
     the ring around the Palace.

Act Five

THE SOVIET MUST SEIZE POWER

354 The Second Congress has opened, and
355 a worker-Bolshevik is speaking from the stage.

THE SOVIETS MUST RESPOND TO THE ASPIRATIONS
OF THE SOLDIERS, WORKERS AND PEASANTS —

356 a sailor speaking to general applause from the congress.

IF THE BOLSHEVIKS PROVOKE AN UPRISING IT WILL
BE THE END OF THE REVOLUTION —

357 the speaker is a Social-Revolutionary.
358 Whistles and scattered applause.
359 Shouts and objections from the Bolsheviks.
360 . . . units run from cover to cover nearing the palace.
361 Under strong electric lights,
362 and to the ceaseless ring of telephones,
363 the Military-Revolutionary Committee is working.
364 Already the circled line around the Winter Palace on the map
     of Petersburg is drawing in.

ON THE ULTIMATUM TO SURRENDER
— NO REPLY FROM THE PROVISIONAL GOVERN-
MENT.

365 A delegate from the Military-Revolutionary Committee flying
     a white flag is swallowed up by the black mouth of the Palace
     entrance, carrying

A SECOND ULTIMATUM
TO THE PROVISIONAL GOVERNMENT.

366 The Red Guard does not attack.

367 The Red Guard awaits a reply to the ultimatum.

THE MOMENT FOR THE SEIZURE OF POWER
HAS NOT YET ARRIVED.

368 — a Menshevik proudly closes his speech and resumes his place.

369 Again whistling and sporadic bursts of applause.

THERE ARE THREE QUESTIONS ON THE AGENDA

370 — the new Bolshevik presidium has taken the floor.

FIRSTLY: ON POWER
SECONDLY: ON PEACE
THIRDLY: ON LAND

371 The second hand ticks on.

372 Time flows and the atmosphere around the Winter Palace is charged with tension.

373 Units of Red Guards and sailors close in.

374 One by one they run in from triumphal arch under the cover of the Alexandrovsky column.

375 The *Aurora* is ready for action.

376 The Petropavlovskaya Fortress is ready for action.

377 Like a stone thrown through the window, a muddied and dust-covered commissar bursts onto the stage of the Congress:

THE CYCLISTS' BATTALION IS FOR THE SOVIETS!

378 The glazed chandeliers of the Institute tremble to the thunderous applause.

379 One by one the reserves draw in towards the Palace square.

380 The circle is drawn tighter and tighter on the map of Petersburg.

381 An officer in captain's epaulettes speaks:

I REPRESENT THE DELEGATES FROM THE FRONT.
WE REJECT ANY RESPONSIBILITY.

382 Whistles, hoots, a burst of furious protest.

THE FRONT IS NOT WITH YOU!

383 And immediately an orderly springs up with the declaration:

THE GARRISON OF TSARSKOE SELO IS FOR THE
SOVIETS!

384 Roars of delight . . .
385 Another telegram:

THE TWELFTH ARMY IS FOR THE SOVIETS!

386 A roar — thunder, not shouts — rises from a thousand
throats:

HURRAH!

387 A thin soldier from the front bounds onto the stage and dins
at the assembly like a sledgehammer, deafening them with his
shouts:

YOU'RE SPEAKING FOR THE GENERAL STAFF!

388 Laughter and smiles from the " intellectuals' " side.

THE FRONT IS FOR THE SOVIETS.
FOR PEACE,
FOR LAND.

389 The Red Guard units at the Palace have moved into attack.
390 A volley of gunfire from the windows.
391 A volley from the barricades.
392 The lamps go out.
393 The square plunges into darkness.
394 The Red Guards fall back, taking cover in niches, behind the
pillars and the column.
395 Silence. Darkness. Uncertainty.
396 With a sudden clatter the artillery rumbles out, crosses the
square and disappears.

THEY HAVE REFUSED TO DEFEND THE PALACE.

397 The workers, sailors and soldiers breathe more freely.
398 Bullets spray the square. The lamps flash on again and
399 again the machine guns rattle.

WE PROTEST AGAINST THIS SORT OF ANARCHY

400 squeaks a man at the Congress, squinting through his pince-nez and twisting the hairs of his beard.

401 In the Military-Revolutionary Committee people chew their nails, shout down telephones and look at the hands of the clock,

402 and at the proclamation which says " 10 a.m."

403 It's well past 11 p.m. on all the clocks, there's no getting away from that.

404 The *Aurora's* guns are primed.

405 The guns of the Petropavlovskaya Fortress are ready to fire.

406 Units of sailors, soldiers and Red Guards are ready to move into action on the signal.

THE SOCIAL-REVOLUTIONARIES AND MENSHEVIKS RENOUNCE RESPONSIBILITY FOR WHAT IS TAKING PLACE.

407 Homeric laughter, piercing whistles and shrill hoots.

WE CALL ON ALL SOCIAL FORCES TO OPPOSE THIS ATTEMPT TO SEIZE POWER.

408 Oho! So it's to be opposition, is it? Roll up your sleeves lads!

409 At the Congress, nothing can be heard anymore over the din and the shouting.

410 The second hand ticks on.

411 The *Aurora's* guns wait.

412 The guns of the Fortress,

413 the machine guns, rifles and Nagans wait.

414 The signals wait.

415 The soldier-Bolshevik pursues his line —

LET THEM GO! THE ARMY IS NOT WITH THEM!

416 The units close in on the Palace.

417 The tension mounts.

418 The Georgievsky regiment is unable to withstand the strain of waiting and surrenders.

419 A worker, a soldier and a sailor take over from each other on the Congress platform.

420 Like " bulls charging at a wall ", they hammer one and the same thing

72

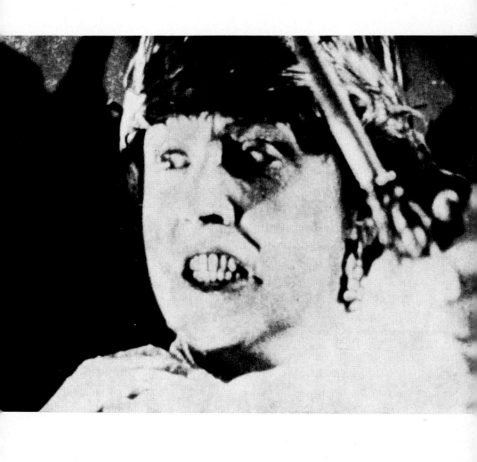

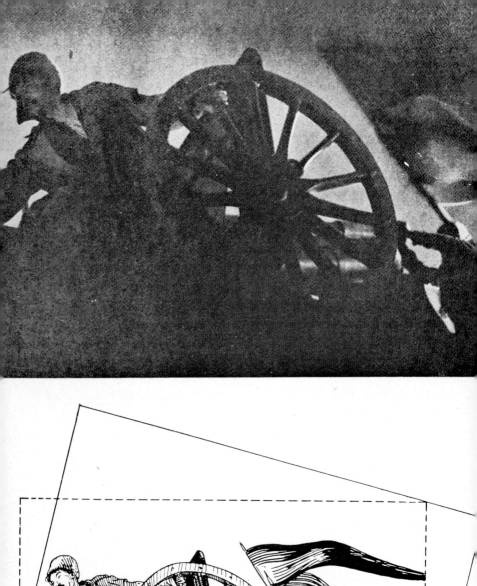

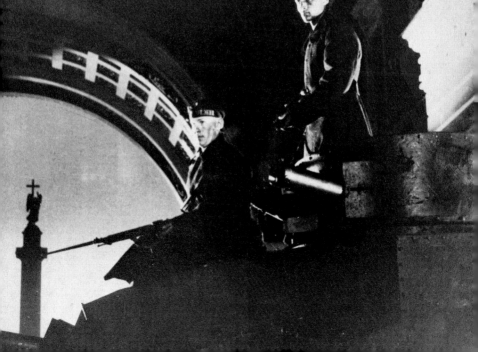

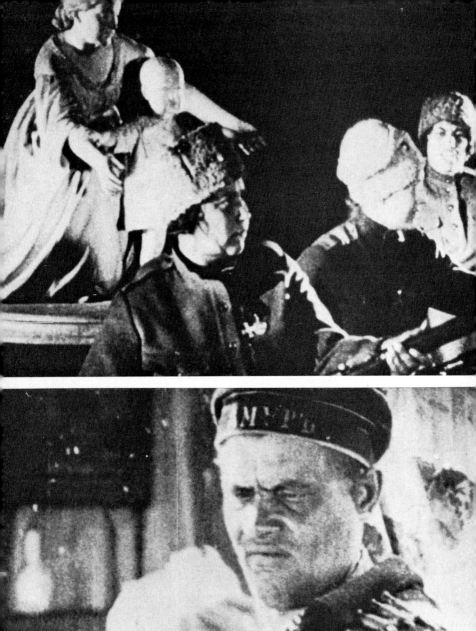

FOR POWER, FOR PEACE, FOR LAND.

421 They are followed by Martov.

422 He wails heart-rendingly:

CITIZENS, COMRADES, PROBLEMS HAVE TO BE DEALT WITH PEACEFULLY.

423 A question on the telephone to the Revolutionary Committee —

NO REPLY TO THE ULTIMATUM — DO WE ATTACK?

424 Guns, machine guns, sailors, brownings, soldiers, rifles, Red Guards — all are ready to go into action.

WE DO NOT WANT BLOODSHED.

425 That's why they wait — Red Guards, sailors and soldiers.

426 Feverishly, trembling with tension, the cadets load their weapons.

THE BLOOD OF OUR BROTHERS IS BEING SPILT

427 Martov shouts, clutching his head in his hands.

428 Whistles, stamps, and shouts prevent him from finishing.

429 Again a Bolshevik " charges at the wall ":

IMMEDIATE PEACE WITHOUT ANNEXATION!

430 Again a Bolshevik hammers out his line:

AN END TO SECRET DIPLOMACY!

431 On the square the women's battalion has surrendered, unable to bear the growing tension.

432 While at the Congress the same line is pursued:

POWER MUST PASS TO THE SOVIETS.

433 Again a furious burst of machine gun fire sprays the square.

434 A sporadic exchange of shots starts up.

435 Fingers drum on the arms of chairs, feet tap anxiously under the presidium table.

436 A clock shows midnight, and there's no getting away from that.

THE DEADLINE IS UP

NO REPLY TO THE ULTIMATUM!

437 Drizzling rain. Puddles on the streets.

438 Midnight.

439 A telephone rings. An order from the Revolutionary Committee:

RAISE THE SIGNAL.

440 Agitation and activity break out in the Fortress; in their excitement the men are unable to raise the beacon.

441 Midnight.

442 The tension reached its limits.

443 The *Aurora*'s guns waited.

444 On the *Aurora*'s bridge someone has noticed the beacon that the men are struggling to raise.

445 The *Aurora* saw the signal and instantly her guns fired a blank shell.

446 Instantly, six hundred members of the Congress jumped as one man.

447 Instantly, Martov dissolved into hysteria:

WE CANNOT DO THIS!

448 The Petropavlovskaya Fortress fired a salvo.

WE WILL NOT DO THIS!

449 The machine guns, rifles and brownings went into action.

THE SOCIAL-REVOLUTIONARIES AND MENSHEVIKS ARE LEAVING TO DIE WITH THE GOVERNMENT.

450 Answering the call, fifty intellectuals fled the Congress like mice, to an accompaniment of laughter, whistles and bursts of gunfire.

THE GOVERNMENT REFUSES TO YIELD.

451 Then came the real volley.

452 Then shells began to whistle over the city.

453 Volley after volley thundered from the cruiser and the Fortress.

454 One shell hit the cornice of the Winter Palace, another a window.

455 Sailors on the roof threw a bomb down the chimney.

456 Precisely into the room where the Government sat.

457 The explosion almost frightened the ministers to death.

458 People rushed out of every crevice into the square.

459 In the face of fire from machine guns and rifles, an attack was mounted on the barricades.

460 The Bolsheviks hammer their line at the Congress to the sounds of gunfire.

461 A group of white-haired city fathers together with the clergy, merchants and public figures, armed with lanterns and headed by the Mayor Schreider, came —

TO DIE WITH THE GOVERNMENT.

462 A sailors' check-point refused the Mayor entry to the square.

463 Shaking his head, the Mayor led away the defenders of the Government.

464 The Red Guard broke their way into the Palace. *(Still)*[1]

465 The cadets fired and threw grenades in the stairways and corridors.

466 A brief hand-to-hand battle went on in all corners.

467 A member of the Revolutionary military staff (Podvoisky), looking rather like an artist, dashed from room to room, leaping over the scattered, dirty mattresses, slipping on the parquet flooring, and ran up to the door.

468 The cadets could have cut him to pieces with their bayonets.

469 Sailors ran up just in time and drove them off.

470 The member of the staff made his way to the room which held the petrified Government.

471 The twelve ministers were surrounded by a guard.

472 Ever new masses poured across the square.

473 The shooting in out-of-the-way corners of the Palace had still not died down.

474 The turbulent Congress meeting had quietened.

475 People held their breath.

THE WINTER PALACE IS TAKEN!
THE GOVERNMENT HAS BEEN ARRESTED!
KERENSKY HAS FLED.

---

[1] Still shows close-up of sailor in the Tsarina's bedroom.

474   Applause burst out like gunfire,
475   Lenin stood on the platform.

        I CONGRATULATE YOU.

478   A tremor passed through the Congress.
479   Lenin said:

        **THE WORKERS' AND PEASANTS' REVOLUTION
        HAS BEEN ACCOMPLISHED!
        LONG LIVE THE INTERNATIONAL SOCIALIST
        REVOLUTION!**

The last shots for Part One were taken on October 11, while Eisenstein had begun editing on September 24. Faced with 300,000 feet of film, the group soon admitted that they could not make a single film of it, nor could they be ready by the celebration deadline in November. On October 12 Eisenstein and Alexandrov made an emergency proposal: that their film (no one thought any longer about the "later" Part Two) be divided into two films, "Before October" and "October", that a preliminary cutting of these two films (13,000 feet together) could be shown to the Jubilee Committee on November 3, and that they could be corrected in time for the Jubilee showings, November 6 in Moscow and November 8 in Leningrad. Fragments of the second half of *October* were shown on November 6 at the Bolshoi Theatre ceremonies.

What took place in the cutting-room and the administrative offices between that glimpse and the public release of *October* (9,000 feet) on March 14, 1928 can only be guessed. Sections of the "libretto" published below were omitted: i.e., the beginning of "Act Three"; and it seems that most of the sequences identified with Eisenstein's theory of an "intellectual cinema" were placed or re-placed in the film at this time, according to people (including Alfred Barr and Diego Rivera) who saw early screenings of *October* without these significant moments (mostly increasing the ironic attitude to Kornilov, Kerensky and the Provisional Government, one might conclude). In this interval, too, Edmund Meisel was brought to Moscow to compose the score for *October* (played abroad only, as was his *Potemkin* music), encouraged by Eisenstein to go further than he had in *Potemkin* in attempting musical parallels to the *ideas* in the film.

Nineteen twenty-seven was a chaotic year for the Communist Party's leadership, and this chaos did not speed the satisfactory completion of *October*. The mere reporting of what happened in 1917 became a task of the greatest political complexity. Consider that John Reed's *Ten Days That Shook the World* became a forbidden book (until after Stalin's death and the 20th Congress), and the greater official sensitivity to the power of film will show us Eisenstein's problem as nearly insuperable. He privately counted *October* among his failures.

The Berlin distribution office changed the title, mistakenly, to *Ten Days That Shook the World* and that is how *October* was shown throughout the world.

ALEXANDER NEVSKY

It was nine years since his last completed, released film. But the popular success of *Alexander Nevsky* in 1938 brought back immediately the nearly lost reputation of Eisenstein. The lost years, the lost films, the lost projects were not to be recovered, but the Old Man was again the Old Master of the Soviet cinema.

The first public evidence of a new film under way came with the publication of a scenario entitled *Russ*, signed by Pyotr Pavlenko and Sergei Eisenstein. This appeared in a literary monthly, *Znamya*, at the end of 1937. The administration of the film industry was still headed by a group of Eisenstein's bitterest critics, and the expected attacks on *Russ* came from all sides. But the unexpected also happened: in January 1938 the entire film administration was dismissed ("mismanagement" was the mildest of the accusations), and a new Eisenstein film, now entitled *Alexander Nevsky*,* went into immediate production. It is easy to imagine that without the removal of the old film administration *Russ-Nevsky* would have joined the other Eisenstein projects on the junk-heap where they had all been thrown ever since his return from Mexico.

As if to make up for the lost years Eisenstein pushed the production of *Nevsky* ahead at high speed. He had always prided himself on efficient planning to cut down production schedules, but since *Potemkin* some outside factor had always frustrated this aim. With *Nevsky* he would show Them. He adopted the idea of a second unit, under Dmitri Vasiliev, to divide with him the carefully pre-planned shooting.† The studio had assumed that the film's climax, the Battle on the Ice, required real ice and winter, but Eisenstein's plan was to complete his climax *first* (a customary practice of his), and with remarkable ingenuity the key sequence was finished by the end of the summer of 1938. A field near the Mosfilm studio was levelled and covered with a solution of sodium silicate (suggested by Vasiliev) and the Battle on the Ice was filmed in one of Moscow's worst heat waves. He was given the actors and actresses of his first choice, and he shortened rehearsal time to a minimum; indeed, at least one of the actors, Nikolai Okhlopkov, playing Vasili Buslai, was shocked by the speed with which he was cast, costumed and placed before the cameras. A great triumph was Prokofiev's agreement, early in pro-

---

* Among variant titles Pavlenko chose "Sir Great Novgorod", and Eisenstein voted for "Battle on the Ice". It was Eisenstein who finally proposed *Alexander Nevsky*.

† There is a foreign legend that Vasiliev's job was political supervision of the "unreliable" Eisenstein. This is an absurd fiction: Dmitri Vasiliev (not related to the more famous Vasiliev "brothers") was a regular second unit director on other large scale productions.

duction, to compose a score for the film that Eisenstein had visualized from its beginning as being greatly dependent on music. The two artists worked so closely together that the music was to determine the filming or cutting as often as the filming was to determine the music. The film was completed five months ahead of schedule. Actual shooting began on June 5, 1938 and ended on November 7. It was shown to the Film Committee on November 9, and was first shown publicly on December 1, 1938.

ALEXANDER NEVSKY

In collaboration with Pyotr Pavlenko
Song-texts by Vladimir Lugovsky

This treatment was completed in 1938 and includes one scene which does not appear in the final film — the fight between the two opposing camps of Novgorod, merchants and commoners, in the early part of the script. Eisenstein's original ending, which was abandoned under a great deal of external pressure, appears in the appendix.

*   *   *

Mournful traces of battle across a Rus[1] ravaged by Mongols — clusters of human bones, swords, rusted spears. *(Still)* Fields overgrown with weeds. Ruins of villages razed by fire.
Rus has been fought over everywhere.
One after another stretch the burial grounds of Ryazan, Suzdal and Pereyaslavl.

On the shores of Lake Pleshcheyev in Pereyaslavl, things are drowsy and still.
Broad, clear waters stretch peacefully between its hilly, wooded banks. Lazy clouds drift over the lake, indifferent to the fresh wind below.
Five men are pulling in a fishing net, their voices answering each other in song.

> *It was on the river Neva,*
> *The river Neva, the mighty water,*
> *There we felled the evil host,*
> *The evil host, the Swedish soldiery.*

New voices join the song of the five. It swells and gathers strength:

---

[1] The medieval name for the Russian dominion which, until the rise to ascendancy of Moscow Rus, under Ivan the Terrible, consisted of a number of separate princedoms. (Transl.)

Ah! How we fought, how we hacked,
We crushed their ships to splinters,
And our blood flowed unsparingly,
For the mighty Russian land.

Where our axes swung, they cut a road,
Where our spears flew — a path,
We laid the Swede and German low
On the feather grass, on the cold, grey earth.

We shall not yield the Russian land,
The invader shall die on our sword.
Rus has risen to meet the foe,
Great Novgorod has risen to fight.

On the bank, two young lads — Savka and Mikhalka — join their voices to the distant chorus, responding with feeling to the stirring words of the song.

Savka: *It must surely be a fearful thing to be in battle?*

Mikhalka (who despite his youth, took part in the encounter related by the song and who now speaks in careless, jaunty tones): *Depends who is leading it. . . .*

Savka: *But when they fought the Swedes on the Neva, you must have felt fear then?*

Mikhalka: *With Alexander Yaroslavich? What was there to fear?*

Savka (with the curiosity of an adolescent who has long seen himself as a warrior): *How is it Novgorod didn't see eye to eye with him?*[1] *He's a strong prince, and distinguished.*

Mikhalka (in the same patronising way, and obviously speaking someone else's words): *The Boyars and merchants are concerned only for themselves, they have no thought for Rus. . . . A fractious breed . . . and so, they fell out among themselves. . . .*

The song flows on.

Not far off, carpenters are hewing out boats. Fishermen are dragging in the nets. The sound of axes and singing weaves through the air,

---

[1] Alexander was Prince of Novgorod when he earned the title Nevsky for his victory against the Swedes in 1240. Disputes subsequently interrupted his reign until his recall to face the threat of German invasion. (Transl.)

which is utterly still, somnolent and bright.

But suddenly the stillness is shattered by a guttural Mongol shout and the noise of a crowd.

Fishermen and carpenters — apart from a tall young man, possibly the calmest and most reserved of all that group on the shore — anxiously turn in the direction of the noise. Mikhalka and Savka even spring to their feet.

A band of Mongol horsemen gallops up to the bank. The foremost shouts:

On your knees!

Carpenters and fishermen drop their work, sink to their knees and bow to the ground. Behind the group of horsemen comes a covered cart, like a palanquin on wheels. The windows are curtained. The palanquin is followed by a throng of Russian captives, women and old men, from whom come sounds of stifled grief.

One of the horsemen approaches the fishermen:

Who are you?

Who are you looking for, uncle? asks Savka.

There is neither respect nor fear in the question and in response the Mongol lashes out with his whip.

Mikhalka leaps to his friend's defence.

The carpenters also rush to his aid.

An ugly fight is about to develop. Already, everyone is jostling and shouting.

Then the tall young man bending over a net some distance away turns towards the din on the bank.

What's the bellowing about — you'll frighten the fish!

The men on the bank fall silent.

The man calmly approaches the shore with long strides. As he leaves the water he addresses his men once again:

Leave off brawling! And going up to the Mongol horseman who lashed Savka he takes his horse firmly by the bridle, saying — as if he were delivering a lesson:

When you enter someone's home you don't attack your hosts!

The Russian's calm surprises the Mongol.

And who would you be? he asks, puzzled.

I am a prince of these parts, Alexander.

At that the curtain of the palanquin is suddenly drawn back to reveal the face of the Mongolian envoy to Rus — a face thousands of Russians know well.

Now that face twists into what is intended as a smile, and the envoy asks with some interest:

Are you the one they call Nevsky?

The fisherman voices assent.

The envoy descends from the cart. A rare encounter. He has heard much about Nevsky. The significance of the name is not lost on him.

It was you who fought against the Swedes? he asks smiling, wanting to be certain nevertheless.

It was, Alexander replies in a deliberately flat voice.

Mikhalka and Savka, lying on the grass nearby, exchange glances. But the liberty allowed a prince does not extend to them. A Mongol kick brings them to order.

The envoy looks the famous Russian over, meanwhile asking:

And what do you here?

I catch fish, Alexander replies with the same curt disdain.

His attitude is direct without being respectful, which is apparent from his whole way of conducting the conversation.

The envoy is all curiosity. He examines the Prince carefully, as if he were pricing merchandise. *(Still)*

The envoy's bodyguard makes the most of this unexpected interlude and quickly sets about snatching the catch from old Nikita, a scene which Alexander watches closely as he awaits further questions from the envoy.

Following the direction of Alexander's gaze, the envoy utters something sharp and the men at once return the fish.

The Mongol ambassador turns to Alexander again:

Can you find no other occupation?

How is this one bad? We'll build boats and we'll trade across the sea.

Join the Golden Horde, says the Mongol as if not a word about the sea had reached him. *You will have great prestige. We need military commanders.*

His manner is unctuous, insinuating, full of sympathy. For him Rus does not exist. He sees only a famous man on a burnt-out and impoverished land.

Alexander replies:

We have a saying — die on your native land, don't abandon it.

The phrase reverberates like a manifesto.

The Mongol bows ironically, gets back into the cart and the detachment moves off.

His face darkening, Alexander angrily watches the retreat of the palanquin, and the Russians being led away to the Golden Horde, to enslavement and suffering.

A sad and humiliating picture.

It will always be like this, until we overthrow them, old Nikita says, drawing closer to the Prince, and he adds: *A cruel people, and strong. Fighting them will be hard.*

But the will is there? Alexander asks with sudden energy.

It's time we did — to avenge the bones of our fathers, replies Nikita.

Alexander is silent for a long time, and then he says for all around him to hear:

The Mongol can wait. We have an enemy more dangerous than the Mongol, closer at hand and more evil, one who cannot be bought off by tribute — the German. When we have destroyed him, we can deal with the Tartar too.

Well, if you say so, the German it is, says Nikita. *To you it's clearer which of them we should begin with, Prince, but to us they're all one scourge.*

The German won't be stopped without the help of Novgorod, Alexander goes on, evidently giving voice to a longstanding idea which had shaped itself into a detailed plan of action in his mind. *We have to fight the German from Novgorod — the last piece of free Rus there is.*

The Prince and the old man stand together in silence for a long time, looking into the distance.

And the fish? They'll get away! Alexander remembers suddenly, and he strides out to the lake and into the water, leaving the fishermen far behind.

Novgorod is lively and crowded. Sails swell on the river Volkhov. The harbour landing is full of movement and noise. The timbered streets bustle with activity.

Merchants are chanting and crying their wares. Artisans are busy nailing, planing and sawing.

Buyers crowd the grain stores and the boats.

All around lie heaps of skins — silver fox and sable — honey, butter and grain. Fish flounder in wattle baskets. These are with the Russian merchants. The foreign traders have brought silks, velvets, shawls, sweetmeats and fruits from over the sea.

Vasili Buslai and Gavrilo Oleksich stroll lazily down the main street. They are Novgorod's renowned daredevils, pride and glory of the town.

The smiths are hammering chain mail and, taking the measure of their customers like tailors, they are making what's wanted there and **then.**

Everyone is busy and in a hurry. Only Buslai and Gavrilo are bored, with nothing to occupy them.

Just then a Novgorod girl, Olga, hurries by the row of trader's stalls looking at the merchandise. Buslai and Gavrilo set off after her.

Straightening up and swinging their powerful shoulders, they swagger after the beauty with the intention of paying court.

The armourer, Ignat, catches sight of them and points them out to his customers:

That's them, the very ones. . . . They fought the Swedes on the Neva with Prince Alexander.

Olga has in the meantime gone up to the trader alongside Ignat's stall.

Vasily! Gavrilo! shouts Ignat. *Do an old friend a kindness. I have here Indian chain mail, sharp Saracen swords, Tartar spears. . . .*

What lies! Gavrilo jokes good-naturedly. *I dare say you forged the whole lot yourself overnight!*

And Vasily, who is following Olga, says for her benefit, dismissing the military wares with an airy wave of the hand: *We've had our fill of fighting. It's time to think of other things.*

Olga bends down to examine the cloth on display and listens to Buslai.

Ignat notices her presence.

Oho! The bulls are lowing, spring's in the air!

The merchant whispers to Olga:

Ah! How beautiful are the girls of Novgorod! How dazzling, lord! Look at these kashmir shawls — who else could do them justice!

Olga selects things in silence, now trying on a string of pearls, now drawing a length of silk over her arm, occasionally glancing at Gavrilo and giving him a friendly smile.

It's possible that Buslai accepts those glances on his own account — even though he senses they are not directed at him — and he carries on with a speech clearly intended for Olga's ears:

We've had our fill of fighting, we've won our glory. It's time to think of ourselves.

Have you heard? Vaska's proposing to take a wife, Gavrilo tells Ignat with a wink and Olga, interpreting Gavrilo's mischievous look, smiles at him again. For Gavrilo too is talking for her benefit and not Ignat's, like Buslai, who continues to aim his conversation at her.

The nanny goat's in the yard, so the billy goat's looking through the fence, Ignat observes.

Ah, I've had my fill of throat cutting. One day's fighting throws me into a melancholy for two days. I was going to make for the Volga to give my axe a little play, but melancholy overwhelmed me, Buslai continues.

You ought to go into a monastery, says Gavrilo, who can see that Vaska can't resist and is already taking an interest in the chain mail and swords, picking out an iron cudgel set with spikes.

I have an affair of the heart on my mind . . . if it doesn't turn out my way, I'll straightaway shut myself up with the monks.

When the bear enters a monastery, it's to kill the calves, laughs Ignat, and everyone else laughs too since they know Buslai well and know that his interests do not lie with monasteries.

Olga moves away from the trader's stall. Gavrilo bars her path.

Olga Danilovna, tell me I may send the matchmakers to your father.

If anyone's to send them, it's me, says Buslai, moving closer to Olga.

Let her give the sign, says Gavrilo. *Let her heart choose. Give us the word, Olga Danilovna, which of us is to send the matchmaker?*

Forgive me, good people, says Olga in confusion. *I don't know what this is all about,* and she tries to leave, but Buslai bars her path and says roughly, with some vehemence: *How can you pretend you don't know . . . why tease the ox. . . . Say which of us you'll marry — choose either one of us. If you want a tall and merry fellow, just give the word to me. If you want someone more staid, and duller, give Gavrilo the nod.*

Buslai steps aside and Gavrilo Oleksich says to Olga:

If you've a fancy to be beaten, yield to Buslai. If you want to be mistress — I'm the husband for you. I have a good name. I may not be tall, but I have a good head on my shoulders to compensate. You won't regret it.

I don't know what to say to you. You're both good men — give me

time, I will tell you in good time.
The peal of the assembly[1] bell interrupts her answer.

The harbour. Storehouses. Shops. Boats. The peal of the assembly bell vibrates in the air.
People drop their work and the crowd surges towards Yaroslav court. Carts carrying refugees from Pskov stand among the rows of traders' stalls. The wounded are moaning, women and children mourn over the slain.
The peal of the assembly bell gives the scene an atmosphere of extreme alarm. People arrive in haste.
A wounded Pskovian soldier stands above the crowd *(Still)*:
Brothers Novgorodtsy![2] he cries. *The Germans have taken Pskov and are advancing on your town. Leave off your trading, Novgorod! Pskov is no more. We were betrayed by the Mayor Tverdilo. The Germans are burning us!*
A second voice supports him:
They are beating the men-at-arms for rising against them, the trades people are being beaten for not submitting with Pskov.
The wounded man continues:
Those who were caught with a sword were beaten for having it! Those who were caught with bread were beaten for the bread! Wives and mothers were tortured for their husbands and sons!
He is interrupted by shouts from the crowd:
The German is a beast! We know the German!
If you shout, they beat you for shouting, if you are silent, they beat you for your silence! the wounded man continues. *Rus is being divided up among the German commanders, Pskov for one, Novgorod for another.*
A city official pushes his way through the crowd onto the tribune.
Wait, why clamour to no good purpose? he cries. *Why lead the people astray?* he says to the wounded man. *We have signed a peace*

---

[1] The *veche* bell was a traditional feature of life in the capital cities of medieval Russian princedoms. It summoned people to a popular assembly — usually a gathering of all adult free males, in some cases with the power to appoint or dismiss princes, and decide whether or not to go to war. (Transl.)
[2] Plural of *Novgorodets*, native of Novgorod. (Transl.)

pact with the Germans, is that so or not, gentlemen of Novgorod?
True! True! come shouts from the crowd.

What if they have taken Pskov! shouts a portly merchant, *and if it does come to that, we can buy our way out. It wouldn't be the first time! We've no use for war, brother. We don't know what to do with our merchandise now. Our docks are all crowded, our grain stores filled to overflowing.*

Crowding around the platform, the merchants loudly voice their approval of this declaration by their spokesman.

Olga springs onto a cart and shouts at the merchants:

Would you barter the Russian land for merchandise?

The merchant replies derisively:

Wait a moment there, what is this Russian land you talk of, where did you ever see it?

Thrusting forward out of the crowd the monk Ananias shouts at Olga:

It's everyone for himself. Your motherland is where you lay your head!

The response of the crowd is both laughter and indignation — their sympathies are still confused and shifting.

Roused to anger, Olga shouts at Ananias:

You lie, you dog!

But she doesn't know how to win over the feelings of the crowd, she is not bold enough to break in on the talk of men.

Then unexpectedly, Ignat comes to the rescue. He pushes his way to the platform and shouts at the official:

Stop feeding me what I can't swallow!

The crowd gathers around him and falls silent.

To you rich it's all one, who's your mother and who's your mother-in-law. Where there's profit that's where your native land is. But for us common people, falling to the Germans means real death. . . . We must call on Prince Alexander to fight the Germans!

The crowd is on Ignat's side. But a second merchant leaps up:

We don't have to wait on Alexander. We must prepare to attack the Germans ourselves without delay. We'll take Domash Tverdislavich, he'll lead us, he's known battles of no mean sort. Lead, Domash!

Shouts of: *You've said a true word there! Give us Domash! Lead, Domash!* from around the platform.

Domash Tverdislavich mounts the assembly tribune surrounded by men-at-arms.

A great misfortune is approaching, it will require great men of us. I am not the one you need, but another — a man with a stronger hand and a clearer head, one whose renown is spread throughout the realm, and who is known to the enemy. . . . And that man, brothers, is Prince Alexander Yaroslavich!

Agitation breaks out in the square. The people shout:

We must call Alexander!

We don't want your Alexander! a merchant waves his arms in opposition.

We don't want Alexander! his fellow traders shout in support.

Domash tries to stem the clamour. But by now Gavrilo Oleksich has mounted the tribune.

We must call on Alexander to rouse Rus to arms! he says. *Otherwise we'll feel the German whip. We'll be squeezed between the Germans and the Golden Horde. Then see how you'll dance! Send emissaries to Alexander!*

Turmoil in the cathedral square of Pskov.

An iron rank of knights stands alongside the cathedral. The reflections of flames dance on their helmets and shields. On the steps of the Lords' Chambers stands the Master of the Teutonic Order — an arrogant knight with cold, stony eyes.

Beside him is the frail figure of the old bishop whose gaunt face, with its long nose, thin lips and sharp chin reflects a sick fanaticism. Behind the Master and the bishop are the German commanders in their ornamented helmets and luxurious cloaks — these are the flower and pride of the Livonian Teutonic Order, its finest assassins-errant, roaming the lands of others, pillaging the wealth of others, flower and pride of " the crossbearing scum ".

In front of the line of knights, bound and kneeling, are the Voivods[1] of Pskov. Among them, bloodied by battle, is the grey-haired Voivod, Pavsha.

Some distance away under a guard of German footsoldiers stands a crowd of Pskov's defenders, their arms bound. And opposite them is a group of Pskovian women and children.

---

[1] A military commander in medieval Rus. (Transl.)

The women are weeping and lamenting, and clasping their hands as they move distractedly around the square.

A fire has already been lit in front of the cathedral and monks in white habits with delicate Latin crosses in their hands are singing their unintelligible psalms in nasal voices. Flames are licking the dark air and the dark walls of the cathedral, as if some fiery wind had torn the dark stillness of night apart.

The Mayor of Pskov, Tverdilo Ivanovich, comes out onto the steps — he has betrayed Pskov by trickery. He says to the crowd:

People of Pskov! The great Master of the Teutonic Order has been appointed by His Holiness the Pope in Rome to rule over the Russian realm. He asks you for the last time — are you ready to submit to Rome?

Among the bound Voivods someone stirs.

The grey-haired Pavsha answers Tverdilo:

Who appointed the cur? Let them first take the Russian realm!

Pavsha's face, haggard from fighting and suffering, is hard and angry:

It shall not be according to your will, Tverdilo. Rus will not fall to the Germans! We shall not be ruled by the Pope. We have defeated you once and we will defeat you again, in good time!

Punish the blasphemer! shouts Tverdilo, beside himself with rage, and the footsoldiers drag Pavsha to the wall. The women start back fearfully.

A statuesque girl (Vasilisa) breaks from the crowd and rushes to Pavsha. *I'm going with you, father!*

Flee from here, Vasilisa! Pavsha calls to her. *Remember our blood!* The footsoldiers push her away, but she can still hear her father's last words: *Avenge us! Avenge us!*

His arms bound, Pavsha is hauled up the staircase in the wall where he can be seen from afar.

Tverdilo shouts from the steps:

Well — do you agree?

The square is silent. The old beggar Avvakum stares stonily at Tverdilo.

The silence speaks, with great and terrible eloquence.

The Master gives a curt wave.

Burn it. Erase it from the face of the earth!

He gives a sign. That contemptuous, brief signal marks the death of Pskov and its people.

The trumpet sounds. The monks around the fire strike up their Latin prayers.

The footsoldiers have dragged up women with children. They snatch the children from the women's arms and fling them onto the fires.

A black-robed German monk hurriedly makes the sign of the cross over them, saying:

Die, in order that ye may be saved!

The defenders of Pskov stand with heads bowed and teeth clenched. But they do not yield, they will never yield, despite their suffering, humiliation and misery.

The Master makes a second motion of the hand. The iron wall of knights mows down the unarmed population.

His bony old arms raised, the beggar Avvakum whirls around in a frenzy.

Children are shrieking and moaning. Women weep. The wounded groan hoarsely. The metallic chanting of the monks is wrapped in a terrible chorus of suffering.

Master! Pskov lies at your feet, says Tverdilo.

The knight looks at him with cold contempt.

This is not how towns are surrendered, he replies. *If you give me Novgorod like this, I'll hang you from the nearest branch.*

Ananias rushes onto the porch and falling at the Master's feet, he babbles:

Great Master, give the order for the rope to be sent!

The rope?

To tie up the Novgorod rebels, Ananias explains hurriedly. *The insolent wretches intend to resist, they want to send for Prince Alexander.*

He is the one, Tverdilo reminds the Master, *who defeated the Swedes on the Neva.*

A faint smile flickers across the thin lips of the Master.

To him, the mention of Alexander, conqueror of the Swedes, is an affront.

The men who can defeat us have not yet been born. And I have princes of my own to spare.

He turns to a tall, thin knight standing alongside him:

As the senior prince of the conquered Russian lands, I bestow upon you, Gallant Hubertus, the princedom of Pskov.

The knight Hubertus respectfully bends a knee to the Master, who has already turned to another knight, a powerful man with the stature of a gladiator:

Gallant Sir Dietlieb, I bestow upon you the Princedom of Novgorod.
Removing his helmet, the knight Dietlieb also bends a knee before
the Master of the Order.

Serve the Holy Roman throne in truth and faith, the bishop says
ceremoniously to them both, giving them his blessing.

The black monk goes on making the sign of the cross with his long
crucifix, and repeating:

Die, in order that ye may be saved!

The white monks chant around the fires. Raising his arms to the
heavens, the gaunt-faced bishop says ecstatically:

*There is but one God in heaven, he has one representative on earth.
One sun warms the universe and communicates its light to other
orbs. One Rome shall rule the earth. . . .*

Fires burn, children and women moan.

Everyone who does not submit to Rome must be destroyed!

. . . The Mayor Tverdilo tells Ananias:

*Go quickly to Novgorod, Ananias, rouse the people against Prince
Alexander.*

The beggar Avvakum appears beside him.

No, your will shall not prevail, he shouts at the traitor and knocks
Ananias off his feet. *And you, Tverdilo, shall be without homeland,
without name, without kindred or posterity!*

The German monks drag Avvakum to the fires, beating him with
their crucifixes. *(Still)*

Go to Alexander in Pereyaslavl! Pavsha's voice rings out suddenly
from the ridge-piece of the cathedral turret. *Dead Pskov calls to you,
Yaroslavich!*

The head of the beggar Avvakum in death agony appears momentarily, shimmering among the smoke and flames of the fire:

Arise people of Rus, arise and attack! he calls.

The smoke stifles his words. But his call is taken up by the crowd.
Arise, people of Rus, — the triumphant hymn breaks out, sung by
the living and the dying.

> *Arise people of Rus,*
> *To glorious battle, mortal battle!*
> *Arise men of freedom,*
> *For our honoured land!*

An autumn night in Pereyaslavl. A room in the Prince's quarters. Savka and Mikhalka are mending nets. Alexander restlessly paces from corner to corner.

Savka glances at the Prince, and guessing the thoughts that torment him, says casually:

We ought to be fighting the Germans, not mending nets.

Go to bed! Alexander cuts him off roughly. Thoughts are crowding his mind and he wants to be alone with them.

Savka and Mikhalka leave. Alexander stands beside the abandoned nets examining the weave of the tow lines.

That's delicate work, he says smiling. *Fighting Swedes is not for you* — and it isn't clear whether he is talking about the net or responding belatedly to Savka's words.

But on this day Alexander is fated not to be left alone. The two young men have hardly left when there is a knock at the door and Savka rushes breathlessly back inside.

Prince! Some people from Novgorod ask leave to enter.

From Novgorod? Alexander asks, suddenly alert. *Let those from Novgorod enter.*

Into the room come Domash Tverdislavich, Gavrilo Oleksich and representatives of Novgorod.

Great Novgorod humbly petitions you, Domash opens ceremoniously, but Alexander is full of irony and suspicion.

Well? he asks, *have you squabbled among yourselves, and is there no one to pull you apart?*

The enemy is advancing, Gavrilo breaks in. *Izbersk has fallen. Pskov is taken.*

Pskov?

The Germans are advancing on Novgorod. . . . Stand for the cause of Novgorod!

Has glorious Novgorod fallen prey to fear?

Forget past offences, Yaroslavich, says Domash. *Pity the orphans. Stand for Novgorod!*

Alexander is harsh in his reply:

I will stand for the insult to the Russian land. . . .

Rally to the defence! ventures Domash, growing bolder.

Defence? I do not know how to defend. We must attack, and attack without quarter.

Seeing that Alexander is close to agreeing, Gavrilo says respectfully:

Your men are a match for the Germans, Prince.
But the Prince is preoccupied with other thoughts, other plans.
One detachment is not enough. We will raise the peasants and then watch! By spring we will have routed them, he says, giving voice to the thoughts which had been weighing on his mind.

A hut near the edge of the forest. Scorched fields. Music and song:

> *Arise, people of Rus*
> *To glorious battle, mortal battle!*
> *Arise, men of freedom,*
> *For our honoured land!*
>
> *No enemy foot shall tread Rus,*
> *No armies shall enter her bounds,*
> *No road shall lead them to Rus,*
> *No foe shall trample her fields!*
>
> *Fame and glory to her living warriors,*
> *Everlasting honour to the dead!*
> *For the home of our fathers, for our Russian land,*
> *Arise, people of Rus!*

Fields long unsown, burnt-out and trampled.
Gavrilo and his cavalry ride by. Black dust billows up from the earth.
Peasants come out to meet the riders who are singing a military song.
Mikula, a peasant with the build of a folk-hero, summons the people with the sound of his horn.
Peasants armed with pikes gather from the huts and the forest and surround Gavrilo.

The forest. Age-old oak trees still unmarked by fire. A thicket.
Down the narrow path pour the first detachments of the peasant volunteer army. At their head are Gavrilo and Mikula.
New volunteers thread their way through the thicket singly and in groups. They stream towards the banks of the river, fill the roads, sing from rafts, and raise the ancient, tattered sails on their old boats.
Old Nikita, the fisherman from Pereyaslavl, an iron helmet on his

head, leads a detachment of his fellow countrymen to join Mikula's band.

The fields are hidden in twilight, but the roads, forests and rivers are noisy and peopled and the songs that strike up, now here, now there, bear witness that the people of Rus are not asleep.

The river Volkhov gleaming in the autumn light.[1] Noise and shouting from the river. A battle between the two parties of Novgorod is in progress on the bridge. People locked in struggle are falling into the water. The whole bridge is a seething mass of struggling people. That side of the bridge which opens out onto the bank covered with small wooden houses, is where the " common people " are fighting. Here the cry is:

Summon Alexander!

On the other half of the bridge which comes out onto the white-stoned Sofia district of Novgorod, the rich merchants are fighting against the " commoners ".

We don't want Alexander! they shout.

Between the two fighting camps is Vaska Buslai. He rains mighty blows, now on one side, now on the other, and it's impossible to tell what he is for or against. He just likes fighting.

The armourer Ignat is shouting as he presses the wall of merchants:

Summon Alexander!

A merchant, coming to grips with fighters from the commoners' side responds:

We don't want your Alexander!

Buslai swings at whoever comes to hand.

I don't want to go to war! he shouts. *A man can't have a bit of peace* . . . — flooring a merchant.

. . . or a bit of rest . . . — knocking Ignat off his feet with a swing and sending him flying into the water.

. . . or settle down . . . this is the seventh time I've courted a wife . . . he goes on.

Just who haven't we fought against, and still there's no end to it!

Ignat climbs out of the water back onto the bridge:

A man on fire can't be drowned, he says with a wily smile and throws himself into the scrimmage once again.

---

[1] The beginning of the lost reel. See introduction.

In the meantime the Pskovian Vasilisa, daughter of the slaughtered Pavsha, is fighting her way through the crush towards Buslai. She fights as well as the men and they fight her as an equal, perhaps without even noticing that she is a woman.

Tverdilo's envoy Ananias emerges in front of her.

Don't attack the Germans, gentlemen of Novgorod, he blusters. *The German is a brother, and he is powerful!*

Vasilisa gives him a blow on the chest and using her leg as a lever, throws him into the Volkhov.

Then Buslai appears.

So, you don't want to go to war? she shouts, landing a blow on the hero's cheek.

My lord! What a girl! Buslai stutters in confusion and delight, looking at her lovely, fierce face.

Someone titters alongside and is immediately plummeted head first into the water by a light kick from Buslai.

But Vasilisa is too carried away by fury to know or see who is in front of her, and she lands another blow to Buslai's face.

What a fine girl! he repeats ecstatically, admiring her bold courage and her fury.

Laughter breaks out around him. Vaska turns, fist raised for a blow and freezes with his hand in mid-swing.

Parting the crowd before her, Buslai's mother, the awesome Amelfa Timofeyevna, is striding purposefully towards him. She is led by Ignat and a bandaged and bloodily beaten merchant. After them come the maimed.

Calm your offspring Vaska, Amelfa Timofeyevna, they complain.

He'll knock us all to pieces, whimpers another.

The stern and sombre Amelfa Timofeyevna approaches Buslai, menacingly brandishing her walking stick:

Aah! You puppy!

Buslai drops his arm in confusion.

Come here and I'll box your ears, his mother says sternly and Vaska obediently and guiltily drops to his knees, touching his forehead to the ground before his mother, while his eyes seek out Vasilisa as she disappears into the crowd.

Amelfa Timofeyevna raises her stick over her son's head, but her arm is stayed by a mailed hand.

Stop, Amelfa Timofeyevna. Why are you shaming my brave men?

107

And Alexander comes into view, leaning down from his horse towards Amelfa Timofeyevna, still holding onto her arm.

Still in a rage, she says:

But just look, Alexander Yaroslavich, see how many people Vaska has beaten to a pulp. Oh! You wild creature! she growls to her son.

Alexander nods cheerfully to Buslai:

Is this the wild Buslai?

Behind the Prince are Gavrilo Oleksich, Mikula and Mikhalka.

Flattered by the Prince's attention, Vaska rises from his knees and bows. Alexander glances around the bridge.

You fight well, gentlemen of Novgorod. You should give the Germans a taste of this, and leaving the bridge he moves towards the rows of traders' stalls.

We don't want to go to war! someone shouts from the crowd.

Go home to your Pereyaslavl, there's no love lost for you here! a merchant shouts.

Alexander reins in his horse sharply. The people cluster around him.

Love or no love, he says, *it's of no consequence. I did not come to you as a lover, gentlemen of Novgorod, I came as a Voivod.*

The assembly bell peals.

Mikula rides into the thick of the merchants and announces with dignity:

Come with good grace, or the peasants will twist your arm for you.

By now the first lines of peasant volunteers have come into sight. Singing and whooping, they pour into the crowd of townspeople in the city square.

Darkness is falling. The assembly bell still summons the people, while the square is already teeming with life. Alexander's men and Mikula's volunteers head the assembly gathering.

Surrounded by his closest companions-in-arms, Alexander mounts the assembly tribune. Boyars and Voivods respectfully make way for him. With Alexander's appearance the square falls silent. Standing high above the people, who know and love him, Alexander bears himself simply.

He is young and inspired. His quick glances take in the assembly. He has been here more than once before. More than once he has fought in argument with the close-fisted Voivods. But this is not the thought which preoccupies Alexander now. He says:

The Mongols have laid their yoke on Rus from the Volga to Novgorod. The Germans are coming from the West. Rus is caught between two fires. Only you remain, Novgorod. Stand for the homeland, the motherland! For the towns of Rus, Great Novgorod, for Kiev, Vladimir, Ryazan, for our native fields, forests and rivers, and for our great people!

Alexander looks resolute and powerful. At this moment he is not a prince, but the senior commander of Rus, victor in battles, champion of the realm. He makes no attempt to refute the partisans of peace, he offers them no argument. At this moment he is one with those who feel as he does, that the time has come to act. At this moment he sees neither boyars nor merchants, nor the partisans of friendship and pacts. He has one thought — Rus is in danger.

Alexander's words stir the assembly.

The crowd seethes with emotion and excitement.

Torches bob and sway in the hands of the excited Novgorod people. And suddenly the shouting breaks out:

Let's go! Let's go! Rally the people, Prince!

The cry spreads through the crowd and gathers force:

Take us all, call us all!

Song rises in the air.

> *Arise, people of Rus,*
> *To glorious battle, to mortal battle!*
> *Arise, men of freedom,*
> *For our honoured land.*
>
> *No enemy foot shall tread Rus,*
> *No armies shall enter her bounds,*
> *No road shall lead them to Rus,*
> *No foe shall trample her fields!*

The Voivods and boyars approach Alexander:

Lead the forces of Novgorod, Prince.

Clouds of breath wreathe the singing crowd. Horns sound and drums beat.

A group of spearmakers shout: *The spearmakers will give a thousand spears!*

We will make five hundred shields! comes the supporting cry of the shieldmakers.

We give five hundred axes! shout the smiths.

We'll lay down our heads! roars Buslai, who has already forgotten that a moment before he had been fighting for a quiet life.

Ignat, the armourer, quickly opens up his shop. By the light of oil lamps and torches he throws his military wares out onto the stall — chain mail, spears, swords, bludgeons.

Take it all! he shouts. *Take it, anyone who needs it, and death to our enemies! Even the sparrow has a heart!*

Vasilisa is the first to run up. She picks out a shirt of mail and puts it on at once. She is followed by the young men of Novgorod who press gaily in to select weapons.

Noise. Talk. General excitement. Buslai and Gavrilo overtake Olga in the crowd.

Gavrilo addresses her:

Well, say the word — we don't have time to wait anymore. To-morrow we go to war.

Buslai agrees:

Why drag things out, Danilovna? Say it straight.

Let fate decide how it is to be, Olga replies. *The braver of the two in battle may send the matchmaker.*

Ignat's shop gradually empties. He's given out everything by now, and finding a poor, rusty chain-mail shirt under the stall he looks at it dubiously.

Well it wasn't a gift from the enemy, I made it myself, he says ruefully, and adds as he measures it up against himself: *This shirt's on the short side!*

The song still rings out over the Novgorod night, a song which is both hymn and rallying cry:

> *Arise, people of Rus. . . .*

The bishop's tent. The bishop is celebrating a solemn rite. *(Still)* The monotonous flow of nasal Latin chants is audible. Kneeling knights pray with an air of self-importance and pride. At their head is the Master. Behind him, the newly-elected " princes ", Hubertus and Dietlieb.

At the entrance to the tent among a group of younger knights, Tverdilo is also praying earnestly. He is still unsure of the liturgical rites of his new faith and gets confused, sometimes crossing himself in the Latin manner, sometimes inadvertently the Orthodox way.

The prayer of the knights is solemn and dignified; they chant calmly, without passion. But outside around the campfires the poorer and more numerous foot-soldiers kneel in the snow and sing the psalms in piercing voices.

The coarse snow spreads mantles of white over them.

Ananias rushes into the tent, covered in snow, and whispers something in Tverdilo's ear. The latter creeps on his knees to the Master and passes on the message.

The Master rises from his knees. He brings the praying to a halt with a motion of the hand. Business with God is over.

Brother knights, King Alexander has dared to rise against us, but God has punished him. His advance army is snowed up in the forest like a bear. We must make haste to hunt down the Russian beast. To horse!

The knights spring to their feet, don their helmets and seize their swords, with cries of: *Vivat! Vivat!*

Alongside the bishop's tent, Ananias examines the trappings of the Catholic service with hostile curiosity. Tverdilo slaps him on the shoulder:

Lead the way!

The dark clearing in the forest comes to life. Torch-light makes the helmets and armour sway. Horses snort and neigh. The footsoldiers and knights assemble in full battle array.

Ananias is already at the head of the column. A dense, snow-filled fir grove. The barest outline of a path in the snow.

Night.

The Russian detachment is making its way on skis through the snow-laden fir trees. In the lead are Voivod Domash Tverdislavich and Voivod Vaska Buslai. They move soundlessly. The snow is as thick as a fog.

Ananias comes into view, parting the branches of a fir tree on the side of the ravine.

The firs shudder. Snow falls softly from their branches.

The knights and foot-soldiers sweep past beyond the frame.

They spring suddenly on the scattered Russian detachment.

A battle breaks out, taking the Russians by surprise.

But no one flees. They fight, even though unprepared for battle.

The clash of swords and the shouts carry into the distance.

A forest on the shore of a frozen lake. Two hollowed-out boats frozen in the ice.

The clash of swords carries to the shore from the distant forest.

On the other side of the lake where the ring of swords cannot be heard, damp campfires glimmer softly. Vague outlines of drowsy soldiers. The shouts of guards on sentry duty.

Alexander and Gavrilo are standing near the big watchfire, waiting for the advance detachment led by Domash and Buslai to return. Around the fire are Mikula, Savka and some soldiers. The hauberk maker Ignat is entertaining them with a tale. The soldiers are listening and laughing. Tired and tense at the absence of the advance detachment, Alexander finds himself listening to Ignat's story in spite of himself.

A vixen from Livonia gets into the way of calling on a peasant. She comes once, and devours his hens to the last one. A second time, and she guzzles down the ducks.

The vixen grows fatter, the peasant leaner. The peasant gets angry.

"Just you wait, you glutton! I'll teach you a lesson."

So he sits down by a hole in the ice and starts fishing. Sure enough, the devil brings the vixen along.

"Good day to you, Pskovian," says the vixen.

"Good day to you, plague take you."

"I've come all the way from Livonia. I'm tired, worn out, starving" (but you could see her belly was dragging on the ice from all that stolen fowl). "You wouldn't have some carp in that sack of yours?"

"Carp, plague take you? Full to the gills and still your eyes are bigger than your stomach! Well I can play that game too. Stick your nose in that sack and help yourself to some carp."

"Gut, gut . . . I'm very partial to carp. Gut, gut, . . ." and she shoves her head in the bag of her own accord.

The peasant gives her a little nudge and traps her in the sack.

"What are you doing, Pskovian? Enough of your games! How could you. . . ."

112

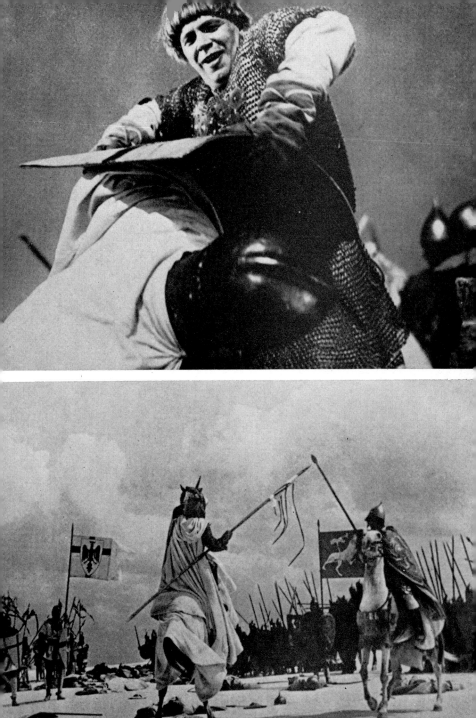

She wriggles and struggles, but there's no getting out of the sack.

"I know just how to deal with the likes of you; I'm staying on the ice and you're going down below," and he pitches her into the hole. *"It isn't all carp in Rus, you know, we have ruffs[1] as well. Forewarned is forearmed, my friend."*

Alexander (reiterating): *It isn't all carp in Rus, we have ruffs as well?*[2]

Ignat (laughing): *Ruffs as well.*

Alexander: *Forewarned is forearmed?*

Ignat (dissolving with laughter): *. . . forearmed.*

Everyone around them is laughing.

Suddenly a ragged and dishevelled fighter rushes up to the fire. With some difficulty it's possible to recognise him as Ananias. He flings himself on his knees before Alexander:

Run, Prince. Save yourself. Lead your men home! The Germans are advancing in vast numbers. They've killed Domash and taken Buslai.

Alexander explodes with rage. He takes Ananias by the throat and shakes him.

Taken Buslai? You're lying, you dog! and he throws him to the ground.

Gavrilo Oleksich says to Ananias:

Buslai would never give himself up. You slander him, and lands another blow which knocks Ananias off his feet.

Alexander leaps onto his horse.

---

[1] A freshwater fish with prickly scales.

[2] Ignat's story as it emerges in the film runs as follows:

> *A hare leaps into a ravine with a vixen on his tail. He makes for the forest, the vixen after him. So the hare hops between a pair of birch trees. The vixen springs after him — and sticks. Pinned between the two birches, she wriggles and she struggles, but there's no getting free. Calamity! Meanwhile the hare stands alongside her and says in a serious voice: "If you're agreeable," he says, "I'll now put paid to your virginity, all of it. . . ."*
>
> The soldiers around the campfire laugh. Ignat goes on:
>
> *". . . Oh, how can you, good neighbour, it isn't done. How can you serve me such a shameful trick. Have pity!" she says.*
>
> *"This is no time for pity," the hare tells her. And he pounces.*

Alexander turns around and asks: *Between two birch trees?*

Ignat replies: *He pinned her.*

Alexander's voice asks: *And pounced?*

Ignat replies laughing: *He pounced.*

121

Prepare the men to ride to the rescue! he shouts at the gallop, and accompanied by his grooms and Gavrilo, he disappears into the darkness of the lake.

A fir tree beside the lake. Two boats frozen in the ice.
Wounded Russian soldiers run past. They are falling and slipping in the snow. Some have already been buried by the snow and only the peaks of their helmets can be seen.
In the distance the campfires of Crow's Rock, the crags near the lake.
Alexander reins in his horse at full gallop and listens. Distant sounds of battle can be heard.
Gavrilo's horse slips on the ice.
What are you slipping for? grumbles Gavrilo.
Hooves slipping? asks Alexander. *This is the place to attack their cavalry, right here, next to Crow's Rock.*
But the ice is thin, Yaroslavich. It will give way unexpectedly, Gavrilo objects.
The German is heavier than we are, Alexander says defiantly. *If it breaks under him, what is it to us?* He gallops off in the direction of the noise of fighting.

Buslai runs into frame. Dazed men from the detachment run past him.
Cross the lake! Buslai shouts to them. *Get across the lake!*
Alexander and Gavrilo have by now drawn level with Buslai. Alexander jumps from the saddle and goes up to him:
Where are you going in such a hurry, Vasya? Are you cramped for space here?
Distracted and confused, Buslai spreads his arms:
These are foreign parts, and dark. . . . We're going back to our own side where it would all be so much easier. Lead the way, Prince, lead the armies back across the lake!
He is breathing heavily and keeps looking around him. The dead are being carried past.
The wounded press on.
Gavrilo Oleksich supports Buslai:
Hurry, Prince. What he says is true. Let's get back before light. Even fighting is easier on your native soil. Every stone is a friend, every hollow a sister.

Scarcely able to restrain his anger and resentment, Alexander says harshly to Buslai:

If you haven't the strength to fight on foreign ground, you have no business on your own, and he pushes him away scornfully. *We are going to fight on foreign ground. Is that understood?*

The body of Domash Tverdislavich is carried into frame. Alexander goes up to the dead man and drops to his knees, silently contemplating the still face of the great warrior, Novgorod's pride and glory. He covers Domash's face with a kerchief.

I will not let the dogs onto Russian soil, he says quietly as if uttering a vow, and after a moment, adds to Gavrilo: *We will fight on the lake!* He calls the commanders to him.

We will range the main force at Crow's Rock. You, Gavrilo, will head a detachment and take up a position on the left. I and my men will take the right. You, Mikula, will post the peasants in ambush at the rear. . . . The Germans will of course attack with the wedge — the " swine " formation. The main force will meet the attack here.

Buslai looks glum.

Who's going to lead the main force? he asks tonelessly.

Alexander had anticipated his question, and his sense of injury.

You will, he says. *You've been running all night, by day you will make a stand. And you will take the full force of the attack. You will hold the German and not give an inch until Gavrilo and I pour in from right and left and pin him in. Is that understood?*

Buslai nods wordlessly in reply. He hasn't the strength to speak since he realises how much of the responsibility for the battle is now his.

Gavrilo goes up to him.

Watch your front, Vaska. Hitch up the transport sleds and place them behind you. That way you'll hold off the Germans better.

True, Buslai answers absently.

And don't forget our agreement over Olga, adds Gavrilo.

Don't you forget it, says Buslai with a confident shrug of shoulders. *What are you gawping at?* he roars suddenly at his dumbstruck men. *Form ranks on the lake. We've been running all night, by day we're going to make a stand.*

From the summit of Crow's Rock Alexander surveys the future battle arena, still covered by an early morning mist. With him are Buslai

123

and Gavrilo Oleksich.

Down below, soldiers are falling into line on the lake under the rocks. This is Buslai's regiment, the main force, prepared to take the Germans' first assault. The squeal of runners on the sleds, the snorting of unslept horses, the murmur of the peasant women on the transport chain, and the sharp smell of wet hay in the air. The women who drove the transport chain huddle close together and look anxiously out into the distance of the lake.

It's growing light. The dim rays of the lazy April sun are feeling their way across the clouded night sky. Suddenly, the knights are visible. *(Still)* Sharp spears and crests of helmets flash in the sun, and the terrible armoured wedge which the Russians call the "swine" comes into view.

The horn sounds in the Russian ranks. Its call carries across the lake. Anxiously the Russians watch the movement of that gleaming, thundering German wedge, driving swiftly and relentlessly towards them.

Here it comes! Here comes the swine! cries Savka.

The knights' helmets glow and redden in the sunlight. Their war horn sounds. Banners lift. The terrifying advance of the column of knights grows swifter.

Agitation breaks out in Buslai's vanguard.

The swine! The swine! shout the men, looking ahead at the knights and back at the Prince, still standing on Crow's Rock.

Sharp anxiety and alarm can be felt in those shouts, but the Prince still stands there looking into the distance as if he were not yet certain that these were in fact those he had been waiting for.

The swine! The swine! — the cry reaches him.

He turns at the sound. His expression changes at once and with an angry gesture of defiance towards the enemy he shouts into the crowd:

And we'll slap that swine on the snout!

Laughter breaks out in the ranks. The Prince's calm gives them courage. He will stand his ground, he will not retreat.

But the knights gallop closer and closer to the encounter.

And still Alexander waits.

But at last he cries: *Now!*

Buslai looks over the field as if he were challenging each enemy to personal combat and moves off to join his men. He passes Gavrilo.

They exchange a strong, brotherly embrace, perhaps before going to meet their death, perhaps for the last time.

Buslai looks around once more, at the lake, at the Russian troops, at the knights and at his Prince, and suddenly rejuvenated, he gallops off to his detachment, taking up his position at the front.

The snow rises in clouds under the hooves of the German horses, and curls like dust behind their column.

The Russians are agitated. What will happen? They glance at the Prince. He is telling Gavrilo:

Wait till the German attacks Buslai, until the swine has closed in — the important thing is, don't come in too soon. Then we'll attack together from left and right.

Alexander and Gavrilo gallop off to their detachments. The knights are very close. Already their faces are visible through the narrow slits of their helmets, with their ornaments of plumes and horns. The armoured horses sound a heavy clank of metal.

The Pskovian Vasilisa, daughter of Voivod Pavsha, has clambered onto a sled and is looking out in the direction of the galloping knights.

The clatter of horses' hooves, the whine of weapons, the heavy breathing of men.

At their head gallops a majestic, sombre knight — the Master — and behind him, the armsbearers.

In the Novgorod ranks men are whispering, gasping, cursing and hullooing, as if they were warming up for a fistfight. Their ranks bend as everyone thrusts his way to the front, and it is more and more difficult to restrain the warriors who long ago grasped their swords and waved them in reckless excitement.

But the Germans advance in silence. The Master, a towering figure on his massive warhorse, gallops at the head of the column with two knights at his shoulder. The footsoldiers run alongside the knights, keeping pace with the horses. The wedge is about to hit the Russians at the gallop and it is impossible to wait it out. Some ten bold men break from the Russian ranks with cries of, *Holy Mother!* and leap out to meet the Germans.

Get back! shouts Buslai, but it is too late.

The iron wedge mows down that handful of reckless men, any left alive fall to the footsoldiers, while the knights do not falter for an instant, their dreadful charge does not waver.

They clash. The wedge hits Buslai. He raises his sword. Four spears strike Buslai, knocking him to the snow. Four knights gallop over the spot where Buslai just stood.

The Russian centre falls back. The Germans penetrate the lines relentlessly, wave after wave. The horns and drums are silent. Men fight face to face, shoulder to shoulder, horse to horse, and they fight to the death. But the wedge thrusts deeper and deeper. The front lines of the Russian force have already been pressed back. Perhaps because the merry, irrepressible Buslai is not to be seen at the head of the fighting. But there he is! Crawling out from under a knight's horse. He throws off the rider in his splendid cloak and leaping into the strange saddle he shouts:

Put some fire into it, Novgorodtsy!

But even without his shouted encouragement, they are fighting with spirit, and without a backward glance, fighting to the death.

By now the centre has been brought back up against the sleds. Vasilisa runs up to Buslai:

Should we move the transport chain away?

No! Die where you stand! he shouts.

But the fighting goes on to its end. A couple of peasants try unsuccessfully to support the soldiers who are falling in among the sleds under pressure from the Germans. The fighting is going on among the sleds, in the sleds, on the furthermost limit assigned to Buslai in the battle.

The first lines of knights have already passed through the sleds. The horn urges on the remainder. One or two more onslaughts and the Russians will flee, broken in half by the arrow-like drive of the German wedge.

The wings of the wedge are reforming, spreading out to the sides. Buslai sees that the wedge is reorganising its flanks.

Hold in the wedge! he shouts. *Don't let them form up again! To sword! To sword! More effort! More. . . .*

At that point Buslai's horse is killed under him. He hurls himself into the fray on foot with a short sword and brings down a knight's horse. The heavy armour-clad animal crashes down on Buslai with its full weight, pinning him under.

Shouts of: *Buslai's dead! The end of Buslai!* break out around him. The piercing call of the German war horn adds to the confusion.

The wedge spreads wider and wider, its charge grows swifter and swifter. The horn rallies and urges them on. The knights are already in among Buslai's men and breaking past their lines. The battle surges like a whirlpool, without plan, wherever anyone happens to be. Men are locked in hand-to-hand fighting. No one has any thought of rescue.

Then Alexander's voice rings out across the lake:

For Rus!

And he comes down like a whirlwind at the head of his men, into the flank of the armoured column, into the thick of that glittering mass of horses, swords and axes. *(Still)* From the other side of the battle the answering cry rings out:

For Rus!

And the detachment on the left led by Gavrilo strikes the trapped German wedge.

Seen from above at that moment, the battlefield would have shown the outspread wings of the German wedge hit simultaneously from left and right by Alexander and Gavrilo's armies. The knights quickly closing their ranks. The wedge narrowing as the Russians move in from all sides. The knights are still strong, it's true, they are not yet routed, but they have been robbed of their freedom of movement and their terrible charge has been arrested.

Vasilisa, watching Alexander, shouts triumphantly:

Aha! We've pinned the devils back!

But it is still early. The full pitch of battle has only just been reached. The final moment of this fateful encounter is beginning.

Alexander and his men plunge ferociously into the knights' left flank.

Gavrilo with Mikula and Savka presses on the right flank.

Buslai's centre recovers slightly and reorganises itself for a new assault.

The German force retracts like a hedgehog.

At the rear of the column, the knights urge on the weakened foot-soldiers and drive them forward. At this point Mikula throws himself into the thick of battle.

Come on men! It's our turn! Let's at the Germans!

A mighty roar rises over the lake.

The peasants in their rabbitskin caps, armed with their axes and pikes, hurl themselves on the column from the rear. The knights in the rearguard don't have time to turn their horses before the peasants are on them. They leap on the animals' cloth-covered croups, knock the knights from the saddle and finish off the fallen. Bellowing with rage, Buslai heaves the knight's horse off his body, tugs down his blood-spattered chain-mail and leaps into hand-to-hand fighting.

Here's Vaska! Here I am! he shouts to his men, running in among the sleds into the heaviest fighting. *(Still)*

A barrel of rough ale stands on one of the sleds. He scoops up a whole ladle: *Your health, Vasya,* he tells himself and, as if this were a steamy July afternoon, he drains the freezing ale in one gulp.

From the bishop's tent on the opposing bank, the battle arena can be seen from end to end. The bishop himself with all his monks and priests, stands with arms raised to heaven, chanting prayers, asking for a swift victory over the Russians.

And perhaps this is close at hand for even though they have the wedge surrounded, the Russians are still unable to break through its ranks.

Closing in tightly, shoulder to shoulder, and bristling with spears, the Germans are successfully repelling the enemy's fierce assault.

The knights open up their wall, part the shields standing side by side on the ground, and let the footsoldiers out onto the Novgorod troops. They are lightly armed for quick movement and they fling themselves ferociously onto the Russian wave, grasping and cutting at the horses' legs, rolling themselves under the feet of the Novgorod fighters, bringing their opponents down on themselves and then stabbing with their short swords.

Prince Alexander has almost cut himself an opening in the German column. Behind him is the armourer Ignat. Each time he strikes a German helmet he says jeeringly:

Good merchandise that — from Lubeck no doubt!

Alexander responds laughingly:

Our swords are none too sharp when it comes to cutting their chain-mail!

I don't know what you're driving at, I'm sure, replies Ignat in hurt tones, but. . . .

Just then the nearest German strikes a sword blow to the side of

Ignat's helmet with such force that it all but knocks him from the saddle.

Phew! The devil! That sword was forged to triple thickness, he growls, as if to justify himself.

The secret's not in the forging — a sword's as good as the shoulder that wields it, Alexander tells him as he turns his fine, swift blade that has never known a miss on the knight who struck the blow.

Hack away — swing away — you won't parry this! Alexander pronounces a sentence of death in time with his blows which cleave the knight's helmet and bring him down on to the snow.

Everything is confusion on the lake — neither columns nor ranks to be seen. The fighting is fierce. The knight's armoured square stands, fending off the crushing onslaught of the Russians who now feel their strength.

His sword flailing like the arms of a windmill, Buslai is chopping down the wave of footsoldiers that has set upon him. His blade breaks in two and he defends himself with the handle.

That's Ignat's work for you, not worth a farthing, he grumbles.

Someone hands him another sword, but a tall knight whose grey moustaches protrude from under his visor, knocks it out of his hand. Buslai backs away under pressure from his opponent, looking around for some kind of weapon, but the persistent knight has already driven him back against the barricade of sleds.

He can retreat no further. This is death!

But Vasilisa has noticed Buslai's predicament. Breaking a pole from one of the sleds, she throws it to him.

Good girl, he says, catching the shaft in flight and bringing it down on the head of the grey-whiskered knight.

The blow crushes his helmet and apparently locks it shut forever, leaving the moustaches pinched in the closed corners of the slit. A second blow and the knight drops to the ground.

And now Buslai begins the counter-attack. He moves against the footsoldiers, brandishing the pole like an enraged bear. He chops them down, beats them, intimidates them from a distance, flinging them to all sides.

With new ardour the Novgorod troops press in his wake.

Gavrilo Oleksich is also fighting tirelessly. Behind him are the young Mikhalka and Savka.

Gavrilo swings with professional self-control, watching over his breathing, the smoothness of the finish and the cleanness of the blow. He is perfectly calm, for him this is work.

Savka is fighting on his right. He is panting with fatigue and swinging his sword hurriedly, awkwardly, his strength spent. Gavrilo. watches over him.

Savka, take your time! Gavrilo shouts at him.

Under pressure from the Novgorod troops, the German footsoldiers retreat and take refuge behind the knights' lines.

Aha! They're done! shout the Novgorod fighters, but the line of knights parts once again and a fresh wave of footsoldiers armed with long spears springs out to meet the Russians.

And again the Russians withdraw.

This time we can't get at them with our swords, says Ignat, dejectedly lowering his weapon.

And indeed, how could they attack them now?

The column stands like a fortress surrounded by a palisade of raised spears. A mighty horseman is visible in the centre, behind the lances and the banners — the Master of the Teutonic Order with his entourage of luxuriously clad knights — the pride of the Order.

Savka is set upon by a band of footsoldiers and all but surrounded. Gavrilo and Mikhalka try to hack their way free to help him.

Take your time, Savka! shouts Gavrilo. But Savka has already lost his head and can no longer see or hear danger.

One of the footsoldiers knocks Savka's helmet from his head, while a second creeps up for the blow to the neck.

Swing back, son! Gavrilo shouts, but it's too late. The sword slits Savka's neck and the youth falls to the ground.

Holy Mother! he just manages to cry before a swift death overtakes him.

Gavrilo Oleksich presses the footsoldiers even more ferociously. Mikhalka has cut his way to his friend's body. He lifts him up from the snow.

Gavrilo and his volunteers press the surviving footsoldiers back against the knights' square. They disappear among the horses and shields and again the Russians face the living wall of knights. Gavrilo Oleksich is almost impaled at the gallop on the points of their sharp spears. They are about to strike his chest.

Mikhalka has seen the danger and throws Savka's dead body onto the upraised spears. Three of them sink under the weight, while two more part to the sides.

We will fight even when we're dead! shouts Mikhalka.

Gavrilo Oleksich is already trampling the fallen spears under his horse's hooves and hacking at the iron wall of knights.

Seeing what has happened, Mikhalka commands:

Hit them with the dead!

The peasants seize the bodies of fallen knights and throw them onto the spears poised to meet the Russians. Under their weight, the spears give and part, the teeth of the iron wall sink to the ground and the Novgorod forces finally penetrate the column of knights. It bends under the Russians' assault and breaks into separate clusters.

Alexander hacks away without pause. Gavrilo Oleksich is in front among the knights. Buslai overtakes him. He is cheerful, crafty and content once again.

I don't see the mark of your work, Gavrilo, he shouts. *Come, show us some courage!*

Here you are! And here! Watch! says Gavrilo, demonstrating. And, cut down by Gavrilo's blows, a knight drops from his horse.

Another falls to Buslai.

Gavrilo crushes a few helmets.

Buslai does likewise.

Then Alexander on his white horse leaps into the very heart of the battle.

Victory is ours! he shouts to the troops. *Victory is ours!*

Competing in their reckless bravery, Gavrilo and Buslai break up the second line of knights behind which the Master and the most senior knights are visible. Alexander catches sight of the Master and shouts:

The Master is mine!

Buslai, who is fighting on a blood-spattered German horse, responds:

What's yours is yours.

And the Prince leaps towards the Master.

Everything instantly freezes around the Master and Alexander. The two horsemen will decide the fate of the battle in grim single combat. Alexander on his white horse and the Master on his black gallop at each other like riders at a tournament. *(Still)*

Pray! Alexander shouts to his opponent.

They clash. Lances break. The horses snort, baring their teeth.

Beside the tent on the lakeside the bishop raises his hands in benediction.
The choir of monks wails a prayer for deliverance.
Crossing himself, sometimes in the Latin way, sometimes in the Russian, Tverdilo peers from behind the bishop, muttering, *God save us, God save us,* over and over.

Alexander and the Master close once more. Their swords clash.
Alexander's blade flies off in splinters.
A gasp from the field, the men freeze and tense — a tension so painful that people seem to have stopped breathing.
The footsoldiers cluster closer. . . . The peasant volunteers clench their teeth.
Alexander does not abandon the duel. He seizes an axe from the hands of the nearest peasant and, standing in his stirrups, he strikes the Master on his mighty iron hand. The German starts to slip from his horse.

On the hill beside the lake, the Master's tent collapses under Ignat's blows.
The frightened monks scatter. Shouts from the Russians carry over the whole lake.
Alexander swings his axe over the Master floundering in the snow. The latter raises his arms and gets onto his knees.
Into the sleds with him! cries Alexander, satisfied, and lowers his axe.
A rope noose is placed around the neck of the kneeling Master — mark of shame and captivity.

On the hill beside the lake, Vasilisa and Ignat tie up the bishop. The monks use their crosses to defend him from the Novgorod troops pressing in from all sides, and Vasilisa joins battle with the monks.
Tverdilo leaps out of the group and makes for the forest.
Ananias follows on his heels.
Vasilisa is overtaking Ananias.
Ignat gives chase after Tverdilo. The forest. A narrow, snowed-up path. The knights' abandoned transport chain, heaped with ropes for the prisoners.
Vasilisa catches up with Ananias and despatches him with her sword.

Tverdilo runs alongside the sleds with the load of ropes. Ignat overtakes him.

The traitor is deathly afraid. He falls to his knees, raising his arms. Ignat throws a rope noose over him.

But behind them the knights' war horn rings out.

Ignat turns. Tverdilo strikes a blow with a cobbler's knife to the opening which Ignat's short chain-mail leaves at his neck.

This shirt's on the short side, whispers Ignat as he falls to the snow.

The horn sounds. Darkness begins to fall. The day is already over. The lake is empty.

Alone a frozen knight stands blowing on his horn, but the battle is far away.

The surviving Germans converge towards the sound of the horn from all sides. They have one thought — to flee, to get to the safety of the bank as quickly as they can. Tverdilo runs with them. But the pursuit of the Russians is relentless; they destroy the routed enemy without mercy.

Far outstripping his detachment, Alexander gallops up to the Germans as they herd into a cluster. They reel back at his approach. The ice cracks.

The Prince's horse rears up like a candle and momentarily freezes on its hind legs.

The zig-zag crack runs through the ice between the Germans and Nevsky. It grows wider and wider, and already the cold black water is splashing onto the ice.

The ice cracks. Staggering and swaying, the knights run across the ice floe.

The ice cracks completely, gradually sinking to one side under its heavy load, and everything on it slides swiftly down the slope. Someone gives a shout, waves his arms and grabs at the sharp edges of the ice floe, and it's all over. *(Still)*

Victory! Alexander gives a resounding shout.

Victory! Victory! — the cry is taken up by the soldiers, guardsmen and commanders who have caught him up.

But one man crawls to the surface out of the sheet of water — Tverdilo. He grabs frantically at the edge of the ice floe. The Novgorod girls from the transport sleds pull him out and drag him to the sleds.

Vasilisa is standing by the sleds captured from the Germans. She looks at the prisoner and flings at him:

You took enough rope, you wretches, we'll have something to tie you with.

They secure Tverdilo and throw him onto the sled.

The bishop runs over the snow-covered bank, tangling himself up in his vestments.

He is old and frightened, dazed and confused.

It's all over. The old man looks around him, listens, not knowing where to run. In the distance he can hear the triumphant shouts and songs. He rushes into the forest. There everything is already dark and silent. But here and there he can make out the greenish points of a wolf's eyes. The wolves are cautiously sniffing their way to the battlefield.

The bishop is terrified. He stops. The wolves, too, settle down near the edge of the forest. They wait patiently. Their prey will not walk away.

The thin, mist-covered crescent of the new moon rises over a bloodstained battlefield, strewn with the bodies of the dead, and the distance is clothed in a soft, blue haze.

Night over Lake Chudskoe.

Corpses lie all around. A vague rustle of life can be heard in that uncanny general silence — the cawing of carrion crows, someone moaning, someone singing deliriously.

The bodies of two knights lie alongside a peasant volunteer whose head has been severed from his body.

The body of an old Novgorod warrior. His heroic white beard curls in the breeze.

In the distance, the glow of torches — women are searching for their men.

The sound of chain-mail scraping against chain-mail as a few dying knights stir. Throwing off the weight of their bodies, Buslai rises to his knees and takes a sweeping look at the field of Russian glory.

A few paces away Oleksich lies spreadeagled and motionless.

Clouds wind around the moon, its light is intermittent and dim. In the distance beyond the lake a glow is rising in the sky.

Wolves howl, sated crows caw. Women with torches swinging now

134

high, now low to the ground, roam the lake. A solitary woman's song can be heard — Olga searching for her suitors. *(Still)*
The field of dead answers to the woman's voice.
Nastasia! someone calls from the distance.
Yaroslavna! Sister! can be heard from the opposite side.
Maria! Izyaslava!
Buslai crawls over to Gavrilo. *Are you alive, Oleksich?*
I'm alive, Vasya.
Can you hear whose voice is calling us?
Buslai helps Gavrilo to sit up. At that moment Olga comes up to them, torch in hand.
You're alive, my darlings! Thank heaven, you're alive! she says with tender joy.
Where are the Germans? asks Buslai looking around the field.
There are no Germans, Olga babbles. *There are no Germans, my loves. You've destroyed them, they've scattered, sunk below the ice.*
Content, Buslai says faintly:
That means we've got the upper hand. Glory be to the Prince and to all of us glory. Our blood was not spilt for nothing.
Coming to himself a little, Gavrilo says:
We fought, Olga Danilovna, shoulder to shoulder, we fought the German fiercely, with a will.
And falling back, already completely weakened, he says bitterly, not attempting to conceal his regret:
I'm dying. Olga is yours.
You'll live and you'll bear honour, Buslai says with emotion. *What are you talking about? Die before the wedding? What are you saying?* and he whispers to Olga: *Promise yourself to Oleksich. He had first place in the battle, your hand is his.*
No, I won't live; there won't be any wedding, Gavrilo Oleksich reiterates with sadness and regret in his voice.
And again, Buslai urges him to a will to life and glory, encourages him with the thought of happiness.
You'll live and bear honour. Get up, Oleksich!
Feverishly, Buslai gets to his feet and lifts Gavrilo's weak, lifeless body, embracing him, dragging him. One step, two — and Buslai himself falls to his knees. Then, drawing on his last remaining strength, breathing painfully, Gavrilo stands up and lifts his friend, but he too falls.

Olga is frightened and distraught. She supports them both. Taking them around the shoulders, she leads them like a mother or a sister, not knowing herself which of them would be spared to her by death. In this way, the three of them, stumbling and swaying, walk away into the foggy moonlight.

The cathedral square of Pskov is noisy and crowded. Down the broad cathedral steps come the clergy, bearing icons and banners. The cathedral bells peal in the bell-tower, stained from the smoke of recent fires.

Clergy, monks, venerable elders, and people — the irrepressibly joyous people of Pskov, many of them wounded and on stretchers and crutches. Everyone is waiting for something. Everyone is looking down the street, towards the scorched and twisted town gates, towards the roofs crowded with children, towards the noise and ring of a great commotion which is drawing nearer to the cathedral.

The clangour of bells fills the air and their copper-winged trilling lends a festive touch to the scene.

Streets. Crowds. Buildings. Unable to restrain themselves any longer, the people surge towards the town gates. Suddenly they come to a halt: sleds driven by monks are coming through the gates. On the sleds are the bodies of the fallen heroes. And at the head of them all is the body of Domash Tverdislavich.

People drop to their knees, bow to the ground in honour of their dead defenders.

The hubbub of the streets and the peal of bells do not die away as they would for the usual burial. Instead they swell, gather momentum and take on an extraordinary grandeur and significance.

Sleds carrying the slain. Savka's body. A woman sits beside him with her legs drawn up — his mother or his sister.

Sleds carrying the slain. The body of the armourer, Ignat, frail and bent, with a gentle and knowing expression.

The widow walks with her hand on the shaft of the sled, not raising her eyes from the dead man. . . .

In their hands, the dead carry candles, burning or by now extinguished by the wind, but still giving off a fine curl of smoke.

The sleds carrying the dead soldiers and volunteers are followed by the knights, tied together in pairs, their iron armour clanking, rope nooses around their necks.

They are led like wild animals by the sombre men of Alexander's guard.

At the sight of them, the people rise from their knees and press closer to the procession. Even the noise slackens and grows muffled because people have no breath left for either tears or joy at this moment — all are choked with bitterness. But just then Alexander appears at the gates. His white horse is hardly darker than the snow and it gleams and sparkles with the drops of sweat standing on its neck. Alexander seems younger today, happier than the rest — not a prince, but a soldier back from battle.

People shout to him. What they shout is impossible to hear, but it is something joyful, proud and warm.

Behind the Prince and his retinue, arms bound, come the Master and two Latin monks with the faces of fanatics.

The people shout and sing, the air resounds with the music of song, the clangour of bells, the squeal of runners and the snorting of horses with the smell of home and rest in their nostrils.

The people surge to meet Alexander. Mothers point him out to their children, the old women give him their blessing, children thrust forward to pat the horse or touch the stirrups. He bends down and caresses them with an ungloved hand, shakes the hand of the old people, nods kindly to the young wives, and bows to tear-stained faces. *(Still)*

A sudden burst of laughter, and people stream towards the sound. Tverdilo has emerged on the street harnessed to a sled like a shaft horse, and beside him in the outside shafts are Hubertus, the " Prince " of Pskov, and Dietlieb, " Prince " of Novgorod. The sled carries the girls who were with the transport chain at Chudskoe.

Tverdilo is dazed. His face reflects confusion behind which there still lurks a hope for life.

After the sled come the captive footsoldiers.

The triumphant soldiers' march is led by Alexander's guard. They are followed by the armies of Novgorod and Pskov. Behind them, Mikula's peasant volunteers.

And behind the soldiers marching in formation, the wounded are briskly trundled in.

People surge towards the sleds, embracing, weeping and scattering offerings. And all this colourful and noisy crowd streams into the cathedral square.

Surrounded by a throng which seems to be bearing him on its shoulders, Alexander leaps onto the cathedral steps. People, people, people!

They are already many, but more are pouring in.

Silence! Silence! . . . people call to each other like sentries.

And silence falls, as if the conqueror of the knights were standing there on the ancient steps of Pskov Cathedral alone with himself, and the whole of Rus lay before him.

It's all shouting and more shouting, Alexander says good-humouredly, *with not a thought for the battle, gentlemen of Pskov and Novgorod. But you may rest assured that I would make war on you too, whip you mercilessly, if you were to let the battle on the ice go for nought. Rus would not forgive you, or us, our want of courage. So remember it well, tell your children and your grand-children. For if you forget, you will be a second Judas — Judas to the Russian land. I give you my solemn word, if misfortune threatens, I will rouse the whole of Rus to arms. But if you fall away, you will be mercilessly beaten. If I am alive I will do it myself. If I die I will command my sons to do it.*

He pauses for a moment before continuing simply and calmly:

And now we shall set up a tribunal, and he looks towards the prisoners.

Before the people stand the Master *(Still)* and his Latin monks. The captive knights. The captive footsoldiers. And Tverdilo, with his " princes ", looking around him with frightened eyes, as if in search of support.

Alexander says:

I am for untying the footsoldiers, what do you say?

Mikula replies:

They were forced into it, what do we want from them?

People run up to the prisoners and begin untying them. The foot-soldiers look surprised and bewildered.

Meanwhile Alexander says:

And as for my lord knights. . . .

The Master stands there with the Latin monks and behind him stand the knights.

. . . we'll use them for barter — exchange them for soap.

People laugh. Voices are heard saying:

Aha! He's a proper householder too!

You're right there!

Alexander continues reprovingly:

You're all ready to be entertained, all full of jokes.

His face darkens. He points out of frame:

But what are we going to do with that?

There stands Tverdilo with the " princes ". The men from Alexander's guard run up and unhitch the two side-horse " princes " and lead them away. Tverdilo remains alone.

Silence. The head of the frightened Tverdilo bobs about inside a collar strung with bells. *(Still)* The people look at the traitor with expressions of loathing. The silence is deathly.

Sounds of quiet weeping start up in the distance.

Tverdilo trembles in the shafts. A woman weeps, out of frame.

Alexander looks sombrely at the square. The sound of weeping and muffled lamentation, out of frame.

A line of sleds bearing the slain. Beside them mothers, wives and sisters weeping and mourning.

There lies Ignat, and there the slaughtered Savka.

A pallid Vasilisa looks sombrely at the dead.

Alexander's face contorts with anger. He shouts:

Let the people decide!

And the crowd rushes on Tverdilo in fury. The people run silently, wordlessly.

Tverdilo lunges away in terror.

People are running at him from all sides.

Vasilisa covers the faces of the dead. The sound of weeping and mourning rises.

Suddenly a lively burst of activity breaks into that hushed, grim scene.

A sled draws up at the cathedral steps, driven by Olga. In the sled lie Gavrilo and Buslai, wounded but cheerful. And behind them leaning on her stick and walking with measured tread, comes Amelfa Timofeyevna.

Olga climbs up onto the steps, to Alexander's amazement.

Prince, she says, *decide a maiden's fate. I told them both that I would love — not the fair one or the dark, not the steady one, but the bravest — the one who most distinguished himself in battle.*

At that Amelfa Timofeyevna breaks in passionately:

My Vaska was never second to anyone!

Cries of *Buslai! Buslai!* from Alexander's guard.

The wounded raise themselves in the sleds and shout: *Buslai! Buslai!*
Forceful cries of, *Gavrilo won!* from the peasant volunteers.

Frantic barracking comes from the wounded in the sleds — they vote
with swords and bandaged arms: *Buslai! Buslai!*

Buslai's supporters are ready to settle the dispute with their fists.

Alexander laughs out loud. Amelfa Timofeyevna goes up to him and
says fiercely:

*Enough of your bellowing! Decide as the people say! My Vaska was
never second!*

Alexander laughs.

Olga looks bewildered.

Then Buslai climbs out of the sled, grumbling.

They won't let a man live or die in peace.

Swaying on his feet, he goes up to the cathedral steps and bows to
his mother's feet:

*Forgive me, mother, if I contradict you and defy you for the first
time. Don't slander Gavrilo. If judgement has to be made then, truth
to tell, neither of us should earn the decision.*

He glances around in search of someone. Finding what he was after,
he continues with a grin:

Ah! What a fine girl!

Vasilisa is standing near the edge of the steps smiling at Buslai.

He goes on:

*Bravest of all . . . was the Voivod's daughter Vasilisa. There was
none braver.*

Voices of the guard, out of frame, shouting: *True!*

After her came Gavrilo Oleksich. This I swear before the people.
And he bows to his mother.

Alexander laughs.

So be it, he says with a wave of the hand.

Olga runs quickly down the steps and embraces Gavrilo who is alive,
but still. Amelfa Timofeyevna leads her son down from the steps.
Buslai, who is hardly able to keep his feet, winks at Vasilisa.

She answers with a confused smile.

Amelfa Timofeyevna is displeased and grumbles at Buslai:

You've shamed your mother, I meant to have a wedding.

We shall have one, replied Buslai.

Why couldn't you be first, you wild creature? Amelfa Timofeyevna scolds him.

I've got my eye on a different prize. Vaska points to where Vasilisa is standing near the edge of the steps. *Take that girl in the chain-mail for your daughter-in-law,* he tells his mother.

Buslai and Amelfa Timofeyevna go up to Vasilisa.

Buslai says:

We've always been able to take care of our own, and takes Vasilisa by the hand.

And the girl who struck fear into grown men in battle now modestly lowers her head. *(Still)*

Amelfa Timofeyevna looks her over carefully, smiles and expresses her approval:

She's a fine girl!

Alexander shouts aloud for all the square to hear:

And now, let's all enjoy ourselves.

Barrels of rough ale are rolled into the square.

Olga sits beside a contented Gavrilo.

People cluster around the barrels. The bungs are knocked out. An Old Pskovian brings Alexander a goblet of ale.

Alexander drains the weighty goblet to the accompaniment of delighted shouts from the crowd.

Vasilisa carefully lowers a weakened Buslai onto the nearest sled. Half-opening his eyes, Buslai tells her:

Now mind! Not so free with your fists at home. . . .

Meanwhile Alexander's guards have brought the freed footsoldiers up to the steps.

Alexander addresses them:

Go and tell all in foreign parts that Rus lives. Let people come to us as guests without fear. But he who comes with a sword shall die by the sword. On this Rus stands and will forever stand!

Alexander's words merge with the approving shouts of the people. The air is vibrant with the songs of the people, it rings with strength and courage.

Arise, people of Rus!

141

The completed *Alexander Nevsky* satisfied nearly everyone. Eisenstein had finally shown us his long-awaited power in joining image and sound. All participants were awarded something of value, and Eisenstein finally obtained the long withheld honours that he had watched lesser film artists receive. *Nevsky*'s effectiveness and success were firmly based on the principle of "attacking the present through the past": the Chinese phrase — it became a dangerous practice in China of the 1960s — is "to point at the mulberry and revile the ash". Eisenstein's own over-bold use of this idea in his next film caused his downfall: it ended his film-making career in 1946, two years before his death.

The sharp political function of *Alexander Nevsky* was recognized wherever it was shown, and caused its withdrawal as an anti-Nazi film after the Soviet-German non-aggression pact of 1939 — only to be hastily put back on Soviet screens after the German attack in 1941. At the time the film was planned, the political parable was to have been broadened to include another potential enemy, but this threat seemed less urgent during production, and the early idea for a conclusion was dropped. This alternative conclusion can be read in the appendix below.

Aside from this major change, the scenario as printed above shows certain materials not to be found in the finished film. Censors abroad often omitted the most cruel scenes of the Teutonic Crusaders' religious leaders. Copies of *Nevsky* newly obtained for foreign archives do not omit these scenes, however. On the other hand there was an accidental omission that has not yet been replaced. Victor Shklovsky recalls the episode with relish: "When the filming was finished, Sergei Mikhailovich lived and slept in the cutting-room. In cinema there's never enough time . . . film people always work under pressure, and they can't even find enough time to splice their shots together. In those last weeks on *Nevsky* the people began to work day and night. . . . With no thought of hours Eisenstein would edit, fall soundly asleep, then wake up and go on editing. . . ."

One night, when he was working on the sequence of a brawl on the bridge at Novgorod, he was taking a nap when a call came from the Kremlin that Stalin wanted to see the film. Without waking Eisenstein the flustered official (probably Dukelsky) gathered up the reels and hurried off to a screening at which Stalin gave the film his approval. Only afterwards did the official discover that he had not shown the reel that Eisenstein was working on that night; not daring to reveal that Stalin had approved an incomplete film, the official removed the reel permanently from the released film, and it has remained hidden to this day (see scenario above, p. 106).

Appendices

Battleship Potemkin
October (Ten Days That Shook the World)
Alexander Nevsky

1. Battleship Potemkin

Extract from the original script for *1905*, by Nina Agadzhanova-Shutko and Sergei Eisenstein; the Potemkin episode was to have followed a sequence on a peasant uprising.

89		Stormy field of grain.
90		Stormy sea.
91		A sailors' meeting against a background of sea. A civilian is speaking.
92		A mother. Barracks. Mother at loom.
93		A peasant in chains.
94	MS	An indignant group of sailors. (On the deck of the battleship *Potemkin*, near carcasses of rotten meat. The carcasses are hanging.)
95		The sailors grow agitated. The ship's doctor and an officer come up.
96	CU	The doctor examines the meat. He puts on his pince-nez.
97	CU	Through the pince-nez — worms crawling over the meat.
98	CU	The doctor saying:
99		THESE ARE THE DEAD LARVAE OF FLIES — HARMLESS. THEY CAN BE WASHED OFF WITH BRINE.
100		Ship's cooks chop up the meat.
101		Cauldrons boil.
102		The sailors seated at tables. The soup is dished out. The sailors refuse to eat it; they push the bowls into the centre of the table.
103		Officer comes in. He orders them to eat. The sailors refuse. They obtrusively munch dry black bread.
104		The sailors are summoned on deck. The commanding officer orders those who agree to eat the soup to step over to one side. (The armed guard is called in.)
105		First, a small group forms off. (Quartermasters, petty officers.)
106		Gradually, others follow, in small groups. Some fifteen men are left.
107		Officer gives an order. The remaining men are covered by a tarpaulin.
108		Officer gives another order. (Rifles are raised, but the guard doesn't obey the order.)

109		Horror among the sailors.

109   Horror among the sailors.

110   The officer seizes a rifle from a sailor. He aims at those covered by the tarpaulin.

111   The sailor Vakulinchuk leaps forward. He grabs the officer's rifle. The officer fires at him point blank. Vakulinchuk falls dead.

112   Rebellion. Settling of accounts with the officers (the doctor, etc.). All are thrown into the sea.

113   An officer flies overboard. He is shouting:

114   SON OF A BITCH! I'LL STRANGLE YOU!

115   Settling of accounts.

116   Dissolve. A sloop with Vakulinchuk's body on board sails towards the shore.

117   A crowd on the shore. Fiery speeches over the body.

118   The speech of a young student-speaker (Fel'dman).

119   The crowd sends him as a delegate to the battleship.

120   On the *Potemkin* Fel'dman addresses the sailors. He is welcomed.

121   A red flag is raised. A vast number of sloops sail up with townspeople on board. They bring provisions, gifts, etc.

122   The sailors tip a sloop carrying vodka into the sea.

123   Meeting on board the *Potemkin*. Fel'dman is speaking.

124   Theme of the title: A LANDING HAS TO BE MADE.

125   The sailors object.

126   Theme of the title: WE WILL AWAIT THE ARRIVAL OF THE SQUADRON — THEN WE WILL DECIDE.

127   LS   Meeting on deck.

128   Dissolve to the empty deck.

129   The battleship sleeps. Sentry posts.

130   The squadron's approach.

131   Anxiety on the *Potemkin*. Action stations.

132   The meeting with the squadron. Muzzles of ships' guns aimed directly at each other.

133   A moment of terrible tension.

134   Slowly the squadron sails past.

135   Outburst of general cheering. The squadron salutes the *Potemkin*.

[end of Reel 2]

2. October

Extracts from early versions of a planned sequel to *October*. Acts 5, 7 and 8 are reproduced from the earliest existing version. Act 9 has survived only in a re-worked version of the script in which it figures as Act 7. These texts date from 1926.

Act Five

What's happening?
Why are the sirens wailing?
Where are they going — the crowds rushing through the October fog again?
Lorries drive past along the darkened streets, splashing mud.
The sirens wail.
Through the town gates, over wet, melted snow, people are going out into the night's darkness.
The sirens wail on and on.
A danger is threatening the precious gains of the Revolution, land and peace.

KERENSKY IS ADVANCING.

The Revolutionary General Staff is working with renewed strength.
One after another, commissars come out of the Smolny gates and head for all corners of the city.
And from all corners of the city, people come to the defence.
Women, workers, sailors, children.
They carry machine guns and rifles.
Boys are dragging everything they can carry onto the barricades.
Gaping trenches and torn carriageways darken the streets.

ATTENTION!
ABOUT TURN!
FORWARD MARCH!

The young Red Guard is training feverishly.
A never-ending flow of men, women, and children, with pikes, bombs and guns, with machine gun belts across their coats, with pots, spades, and axes, moves over the pavements and bridges.
The Military-Revolutionary Committee is in constant day and night session.
Electric lights sting their tired eyes.
The military troika issues a constant stream of instructions.
A telephone number is spoken into the receiver.

Contact with the factory.
A Red Army unit moves swiftly out through the factory gates.
Another telephone number.
Contact with the motor base.
Snorting smoke, armoured vehicles roll out of the garage gates.
Another number.
Contact.
A unit of women workers armed with shovels strides towards the city gates.
Workers in the armament factories pick up rifles.
A telephone call from the Smolny.
And the reply:

> ARE THE GUNS READY?
> THERE ARE NO HORSES.
> THE GUNS ARE VITAL!

The factory workers themselves drag the guns out onto the street.
Moving swiftly, unit after unit comes out of the Smolny gates and disappears from sight (from the light into darkness).
People who have dropped from exhaustion are sleeping in the spit-spattered long corridors, in the stuffy rooms and great halls.
They sleep without releasing hold of their rifles.
The relief guard has arrived at the telephone exchange.
The officer in command produces the Smolny's credentials.
A tired guard hands over the rifles.
Epaulettes flash.
Cadets dressed as Red Guards pull out Nagans and arrest the tired guard.
Cossack units have advanced unhurriedly and are pushing forward without meeting any opposition.
General

KRASNOV

rides out on horseback.
Meeting no opposition, the Cossack armies press on along the muddy, autumn road

FROM GATCHINA TO TSARKOE.

Saluting and splashing mud, Kerensky drives past in a car.
The cadets have locked up the guard under a sentry and taken off their "lousy" disguises; they now enter the switchboard room in full splendour, a French officer at their head.
The telephonists' eyes immediately take on a languorous expression.

They immediately show the cadets the bunch of wires that connect the exchange to the Smolny.
Austrian bayonets[1] sever the nerves of the Smolny.
At the Revolutionary General Staff, the telephones stop ringing immediately.
Immediate activity breaks out in the unit near the gates.
Lorries immediately fill up with people dragged from their sleep.
Antonov-Ovseyenko moves in to check the guard and falls into the trap like a mouse.
The Soviet units catch sight of the Cossacks and take cover.
A gun shot rings out. It sets off an exchange of fire.

> STAND FIRM AT YOUR POSTS AS I
> MYSELF AM STANDING AT MINE.

So wrote Kerensky in his orders.
And he stood like Napoleon on the balcony of the Pulkovsky observatory.
Kerensky's guns open fire.
The cavalry move into attack.
The dead telephone lines.
The severed " nerves ".

RATS ON THE HOME FRONT

The dark palace of the Engineering Corps.
Headquarters of the cadet unit.
Vehicles come and go.
Units of cadet officers drive out; Red Cross vans carry out loads of armed and perfectly healthy men.

> THE CADETS HAVE RISEN AGAINST THE WILL OF THE CONGRESS AND THE SOVIETS.

The Cossack artillery has driven the Soviet armies from their positions and now moves off at the gallop to occupy new positions.
In a room marked No 67, with a plate reading " Class Mistress "[2] on the door, the Council of People's Commissars' decree is being signed.
        (Insert decree here)
Women workers are straining with all their might, digging trenches in the damp ground.

---

[1] The bayonet used by the Austrian Army of 1914-1917 had a very broad blade as distinct from the three-edged Russian weapon.
[2] The title *Klasnaya dama* (" Class Mistress ") is pre-revolutionary. Its occurrence here recalls the fact that the Smolny was a girls' institute before it became the Bolshevik Party's headquarters. (Transl.)

151

Infantry divisions carrying Soviet banners move swiftly through the town gates.

Cab horses are unhitched in the streets.

They are harnessed to guns and driven off at a gallop in the wake of the army.

ON TWO FRONTS.

Foaming horses and sweating people bring the guns up to the positions.

Units run through the streets towards the telephone exchange.

The cadets greet them with a salvo.

The languid telephonists are terrified.

A wounded Red Guard drops on the hard, wet asphalt.

A Red Cross van drives past.

Arriving on the other side of the barricades, it deposits a fresh unit of cadets.

On the battle front, machine-guns rattle, rifle shots ring out.

Printing machines are working urgently to put out the Council of People's Commissars' decrees on PEACE.

(Insert decrees here.)

The Cossacks advance.

The first salvo is fired by the Soviet artillery.

Taken by surprise, Kerensky's army falls back in panic.

Slowly but surely, the Red Guard moves in towards the telephone exchange.

Taking cover behind chimneys on the roofs, and behind kerbstones on the carriageways, they creep forward, closing the circle.

A telephonist reads out a telegram just received:

REINFORCEMENTS ON WAY —

For which she receives a volley of hand kisses.

Reducing speed at the corners, an armoured-car nears the exchange.

The sailor Dybenko stealthily approaches the Palace of Gatchina, where he is immediately surrounded by Cossacks.

The Prime Minister gives General Krasnov's hand a prolonged shake and tells him, his voice trembling:

GENERAL, I AM DEPENDING ON YOU.

The Cossacks drag Dybenko into the barracks.

The cadets open the gates of the telephone exchange.

The armoured-car drives in and once inside, spits lead at the traitors in their gleaming uniforms.

Like a flock of birds, the cadets race up the staircases.

The hysterical telephonists start to flap about like fish on dry land.

152

into cupboards, closets, chests, onto the roof.

Bayonets drawn, the Soviet units make for the narrow doorway.

Hurriedly, the cadets change into telephonists' uniforms, into their cheap, modish coats, into repairmen's jackets, and back into those " lousy " Red Guard tunics.

The crowd from the street squashes through the narrow doorway like meat through a mincer.

The tramp of sailors',

workers' and soldiers' boots thunders through the corridors.

Flinging open the doors, the tired, blood-stained and triumphant sailors and workers come face to face with the girls clustering in a heap in the corner and ready to be killed by Bolshevik " brutality ".

Faced with them, the Red Guards back away in confusion.

The commissar from Smolny makes an effort to rise above the general embarrassment and says politely:

> YOU HAVE BEEN EXPLOITED, BUT THAT'S OVER NOW.
> AS WORKERS YOU WILL BE GIVEN HIGHER WAGES
> AND A SHORTER WORKING DAY.
> GO BACK TO YOUR POSTS AND CARRY ON WORK IN PEACE.

Spitting in the worker's face, a hysterical telephonist shrieks NO!!!

The crowd parts and lets the furious saboteurs out.

The arrogant, fashionable girls leave the telephone exchange.

Six " badly dressed " ones remain.

The Smolny commissar calls on volunteers and random people from the crowd:

Soldiers, women-workers, cobblers — they all sit down at the switchboards.

An emergency tribunal is held at the gates of the telephone exchange. By torchlight, and before a crowd of people, speaker after speaker condemns the cadets.

> DEATH TO THE TRAITORS!

Antonov-Ovseyenko, who is wearing a hat and looks like an artist, persuades the crowd:

> THEY HAVE SURRENDERED. THE REVOLUTION SHOULD NOT
> KILL ITS PRISONERS.

A thousand eyes glow with rage.

The white door of the room marked " Class Mistress " barely has time to swing shut before it is pushed open again.

The rotary presses are running off a decree

ON THE SUSPENSION OF THE DEATH
PENALTY AT THE FRONT.

An American,[1] a worker, and a sailor, deliver thunderous speeches on
the steps of the telephone exchange.
The frightened cadets in their women's coats swear to the people twice
over:

WE WON'T DO IT AGAIN!

In the barracks, the bewhiskered sailor Dybenko is telling the Cossacks

WHAT KERENSKY AND HIS GENERALS ARE FIGHTING FOR.

In the Palace of Gatchina, Kerensky follows imperial tradition and signs
over power to Avksent'ev[2] (just in case).
Dybenko climbs the staircase of Gatchina with a merry group of
Cossacks.
As he pauses at a window to check the barrel of his rifle, he catches sight
of a woman walking across the courtyard.
He pays no attention, and bursts into the Minister's office.
But that woman — a Red Cross nurse — was in fact the same Prime
Minister who wrote

STAND FIRM AT YOUR POSTS AS I STAND AT MINE.

Bonaparte in a skirt, runs for cover in the garden like a fox.
The six telephonists who have joined the revolutionaries are teaching
their operators' skills to cobblers, cleaners, carpenters — how to make
contact,
nerve by nerve,
telephone by telephone,
with the turbulent flow of life.
The repairmen solder the line to Smolny.
The saboteurs — the fine young ladies — pick up their boots and make
a haughty exit, noses in the air, knocking over chairs as they go.
At the Ministry, the clerks are rising noisily to their feet — abandoning
their posts.

---

[1] Eisenstein has in mind John Reed (1887-1920), author of *Ten Days That
Shook the World,* or Albert Rhys Williams, an observer of the October
events whom Eisenstein knew personally.
[2] N. D. Avksent'ev (1878-1943) was one of the leaders of the Social-Revolutionary Party and the President of the "Council of the Republic" in the
pre-revolutionary days of 1917.

Two figures remain in that enormous room with its empty tables.

THE GUARD AND THE PEOPLE'S COMMISSAR.

White hands hide away valuables.
Hands in stiff cuffs hide away money.
Beringed hands drop the keys of cupboards, which have survived the burning, down the sink.
Down the long ministerial corridor walks a woman, carrying a portfolio.[1]

THE PEOPLE'S COMMISSAR FOR SOCIAL SECURITY.

The clerks come out of all the doors and leave, making way for the woman.
In the vestibule, they put on their capes, laughing.
Still laughing, they hold out a foot to the hall-porter to have their galoshes put on.
Hungry women stand in queues.
Hungry children stand in sheltered corners.
Hungry veterans on crutches.

THE MINISTER FOR FOREIGN AFFAIRS

arrives at the Ministry to find twelve couriers in gleaming buttons and heaps of torn papers.
The Smolny presses are printing

THE DECREE ON THE STRUGGLE AGAINST SABOTAGE.
THE DECREE ON THE NATIONALISATION OF THE BANKS.

Smolny sends the forces it has at its disposal to the Ministry of Trade. Commissars and half-educated revolutionaries put their whole hearts into picking at Remingtons and sweating over affairs in the enfilades of the Anichkov Palace, in an urgent attempt to set the work of

THE MINISTRY OF TRADE

under way.
On the Nevsky,
naval officers with no epaulettes on their uniforms are approached by girls with ribbons in their hair, who gaze into their faces with naive coquetry and ask them to make a sacrifice

ON BEHALF OF THE SABOTAGING CLERKS.

---

[1] This is a reference to Alexandra Kollontai (1872-1952), a member of the Bolshevik Party's Central Committee, appointed People's Commissar for Social Security in November 1917.

In a thousand ministerial rooms — tables gathering dust.
And piles of torn paper.
Empty cupboards which survived burning stand there like sarcophagi.

COUNTESS PANINA[1] TOOK 150,000 (RUBLES) . . .

from the hungry veterans, from children and the aged.
The cadets are changing into soldiers' uniforms, ruffling their hair up into
a Cossack forelock, and making themselves scarce, following the example
set by public figures.
In the city Duma,
refuge of affronted intellectuals,
before a room packed with rascals,
the saboteurs cross themselves and swear before God their

LOYALTY TO SABOTAGE.

Disguised as Cossacks, the cadets flee to the Don.
Masquerading as seriously ill, the " public figures " drive out of the city.
Ever new representatives of sabotage activity swear allegiance to God
and country on the rostrum of the Duma.
In the Smolny, new delegates arrive constantly to join forces.
In the Duma, a telephonist hysterically tells of the atrocities at the tele-
phone exchange.
And as evidence, all the languid victims of " violence " come onto the
platform.
The bent backs of women — women-workers, women-revolutionaries,
stitching funeral flags in the huge, half-lit hall of the Moscow Soviet.
Enormous flags, and bold letters, expressing grief at the huge losses.
The flags wave triumphantly over the heads of a crowd many-thousand
strong, against a background of snow-covered roofs.
500 coffins, 500 heroes of the Revolution; to the flowing, autumnal
strains of the funeral march, they are lain side by side in a fraternal
grave. The grave is filled by 200 people wielding 200 shovels.

BUT WHAT ABOUT THE KILLERS?

They have gathered at the

CONGRESS OF THE DON COSSACK KRUG[2]

---

[1] Countess S. V. Panina gave considerable financial support to the bourgeois
political parties in 1905-1917, and was a supporter of Kerensky's Government. She emigrated after the October Revolution.
[2] A counter-revolutionary organisation of Don Cossacks in the period 1917-
1918. (In fact the Cossack Krug — a kind of tribally-based parliament repre-

with its bouquet of aiguillettes, badges, crosses and medals,
lacquered boots, and officer's monocles,
general's epaulettes,
ataman's stripes.
The fleeing cadets and their officers, beards shaven, arrive at that
Congress.

> PUTTING THEIR FAITH IN THE LARGE LANDOWNING
> SECTOR OF COSSACKDOM . . .
> IN THE NAME OF THE FATHERLAND

the gold-braided cadet forces begin to assemble.
In Revolutionary Petrograd
a noisy, joyful procession is in progress; feet crunch on the fresh snow
under the dancing light of torches.
It is joyful because

> THE PEASANT CONGRESS[1] HAD RECOGNISED THE SOVIETS.

Because worker and peasant hands have joined in a brotherly handshake.
The Soviet in session in the Smolny is suddenly rocked by the sound
of a band blaring out in its corridors.
A grey-bearded peasant, bowing in the four directions, places a peasant
flag next to the flags of the workers' deputies and, his face flushed,
embraces a burly sailor.
From that moment the Soviet became the Soviet of Workers, Soldiers
and Peasants' Deputies.

Act Six

The Don Army Krug did its work.
A whip lash across the face.
Cavalry swords, machine guns, lances, artillery.

> SO YOU WANTED LAND DID YOU, YOU SCUM!

The smash of a fist in the face,
on the nose, the ear, the belly under the belt.

---

senting the Cossacks of a given area — had much earlier origins. It had
however, lapsed with the Tsarist trend towards whittling away Cossack
autonomy, and was re-instituted by the Provisional Government. The Don
Cossack Krug, led by Ataman General A. M. Kaledin, was the most important of these organisations. [Transl.])

[1] Also referred to as the Extraordinary All-Russian Congress of the Council
of Peasants' Deputies, and held in Petrograd on November 23-December
8, 1917.

GET OFF THE COSSACK LANDS!

Children, old people, women
are cut down by Cossack sabres.
Soldiers and poor Cossacks are fighting the rich Cossacks and the cadet officers.
Abandoning their properties, the poor families flee — in carts and wagons, with their children and their aged.
A wagon flying onto the bridge at a gallop nose-dives into it, breaking its front axle.
The roadway is jammed with wagons.
The stronger fight their way to the front to save their own skins, they fight with pikes, whips and axes — and they block up the road still more.
An army officer comes down from his position and scatters the people with his machine gun. He pushes the wagon which has stuck fast into the water and the stream moves off at the gallop — its carts harnessed to oxen, horses and men.
The Soviet infantry covers their retreat.
The dismounted Cossacks launch an attack.
The Cossacks curse the soldiers.
Frothing at the mouth, the enemies swear at each other, brandishing their fists.
The cursing turns to action.
Rifles are flung down and fists start to fly.
A cadet officer runs in among the soldiers firing his Nagan, but he can't induce the Cossacks to draw their swords.
The captains of the Red units join in the fist fight.
The officer runs up to one pair — both of them Cossacks, one " red ", the other " white ".
They're brothers.
Recognizing each other, they shake hands and embrace.
The officer lashes out with his whip and roars at the White Cossack.
The White comes to his senses and strikes his brother a blow in the face with his fist.
A troop of cavalry comes to the Cossacks' rescue.
The Soviet armies fall back.
The petrol-soaked bridge flares up like a firework.

HAVING DRIVEN THE POOR PEASANTS OUT OF THE STANITSA[1]

The Cossacks hunt out the old men who didn't manage to get away.

---

[1] A Cossack village.

They hang their bodies high on the shafts of the irrigation wells.
Their bayonets slash

THE DECREE ON LAND.

They rip the Soviet slogans to shreds and wrap them like footcloths on the old men's feet.
They set fire to the huts of the fleeing poor.
Slackening their mad pace, the stream of refugees flows down the broad road.
At every branch road more and more people swell the stream.
Men in a variety of dress, wiping their bloody and battered faces, gather in a clearing among the windmills.

THE CAPTAINS OF THE RED UNITS.

They look around them.
Columns of black and white smoke stand on the horizon.
The abandoned *stanitsas* are burning around them.
A stream of carts and wagon-loads of panic-stricken people flow in from various directions towards the windmill where the captains have assembled.
Once they have gathered together, the people start to shout, setting up a form of

MEETING.

High over the sails of the windmills

THE ELECTED COMMANDER OF THE SOVIET FORCES.[1]

appears, wearing a muddy straw hat.
The crowd quietens and the commanding officer tells them

THERE'S NO GOING BACK.

Around them, the *stanitsas* are burning.

COSSACK AND CADET FORCES ARE ADVANCING FROM ALL SIDES.

Carts ride in from all sides.
People rush in along every path.

---

[1] This character bears some relationship to Kozhukha, hero of A. S. Serafimovich's novel *Zhelezniy Potok*. The prototype of Serafimovich's hero was E. I. Kovtyukh, commander of the vanguard of the Taman army. Acts 6 and 7 of this script deal with the progress of this " iron stream " but the interpretation is the authors' own.

WE HAVE TO MAKE OUR WAY TO JOIN THE MAIN SOVIET ARMIES.

At that, the commander of the Soviet forces is almost killed by the crowd.

WHAT ABOUT OUR LANDS? OUR UNHARVESTED WHEAT?

Drawing their Nagans, the captains look sadly at the enraged crowd.

WHOEVER DOES NOT WANT TO FIGHT LET HIM GIVE US HIS BOOTS AND GO AND PUT HIMSELF IN THE PAWS OF THE COSSACKS,

says the officer in the straw hat.

THOSE WHO WILL JOIN THE DEFENCE OF THE SOVIETS, STEP TO THE LEFT!

For a long time the crowd wavers undecidedly. Suddenly they all move to the left.

ALL THOSE CAPABLE OF BEARING ARMS, FORM RANKS.

The Cossacks were hurriedly re-building the burnt bridge.

WE MUST LEAVE IN AN ORGANISED WAY —

continues the man in the straw hat.

CHOOSE YOUR LEADERS — CHOOSE ONCE AND FOR ALL. AFTER THAT THEY WILL HAVE THE SAY OVER LIFE AND DEATH.

The peasant woman whose cart the officer had pushed off the bridge — a woman who had hated him in that instant,
a woman who had realised his strength as everyone crossed to safety over the cleared bridge.
That woman now runs up to the steps and points to him.
staring fixedly at him,
remembering his figure on the bridge.
A forest of hands rises — the crowd has appointed him to decide over life and death.
All the hands are lowered.
One hand —
the hand of the commanding officer is raised.

WE MUST MOVE OFF QUICKLY.

The unit captains tense, whispering in each other's ear.

160

Suddenly they start to gesticulate and shout from the height of the steps into the crowd:

WE NEED TO REST.

The man in the straw hat raises his head and cuts them off angrily.

AM I IN COMMAND, OR ARE YOU?

The captains lower their heads, come down from the steps and give the order to their sections.

One thousand wagons loaded with domestic chattels move slowly off the spot, stretching out into a long line down the winding road.

The commander issues orders.

Machine guns drive the Cossacks from the half-resurrected bridge.

A captive officer is brought up to the commander.

Cart after cart joins on to form the tail of an enormous wagon train.

The prisoner proves to be that same officer who had urged the brothers to fight each other.

To one side of the steady flow of carts, a unit raises its rifles to shoot the cadet.

A grey-bearded old man jumps down from a cart. He has seen the officer. He shouts to the soldiers who were just about to fire.

STOP! THAT'S MY SON!

The son's eyes light up.

The old man asks the soldiers to wait.

Then, tearing off his son's epaulettes, he shoots him with his hunting rifle.

The head of that endless, moving column of carts is lost in the dusty distance.

At the head of the stream of people, the Red units carry banners

LONG LIVE SOCIALISM!
LONG LIVE THE WORKERS!

Soldier after soldier moves up to the front.

Every soldier has a mother, wife, sweetheart, children in the wagon train.

Every soldier has abandoned his land to the whim of the Cossacks.

Every cart has been hastily loaded with the " wealth " of the peasant:

pillows, blankets,

sewing machines,

cheap wall clocks,

pots, pans,

mirrors, hens — and pillows and more pillows.

In the wake of every cart trudges the tethered stock,
cows,
goats,
pigs,
dogs.
Soldiers' bayonets bristle on all sides.
Soldiers move ahead in any way they can.
Washing is spread to dry on the bayonets .
Cradles are strung on the gun carriages.
Boots are hanging out to air on the rifles.
In the crowd of fighters there are
genuine soldiers in tunics and fur hats,
genuine, mounted Cossacks in circassian coats.
But there are also a great number of fishermen, barbers, workers, coopers,
smiths, carpenters and peasants in motley dress.
The stream makes its way to join the Red armies, towards the pass
through the ridge of Caucasian mountains, its numbers constantly
swelled by new units —
through the cultivated fields of unharvested Kuban wheat, through the
steamy July weather.
Carving their way through the abundant black earth of Kuban, the
crowd of thousands leaves desolation in its wake, like a creeping horde
of wingless locusts.

Act Seven

TO JOIN THE RED ARMIES

Two hundred thousand poor peasants driven out of the Kuban roll along
the winding mountain roads to the pass.

THE SIXTH WEEK.

The stream moves steadily on for the second month, halting only to rest
a little and to water the horses.
The water in the casks is drying up, the horses are watered on grape
juice.
The last of the bread is eaten by the exhausted children.
The old people and the women, as they pass, snatch fruit and greenstuff
to fill their stomachs.
The soldiers grow thinner and tighten the belts of their trousers.
From the height of the pass, the sea suddenly rises in front of them like
a high wall.
Crossing over the summit, the stream flows more quickly over the loop-

ing road that runs down to the sea.

In the bay at the end of the road the battleship *Geben* lies at anchor with some Turkish minelayers.

The German commander sees the horde descending from the mountains and sends out a mounted patrol in gleaming helmets.

In icy-cold and worn-out Moscow, in the half-lit hall of the Hotel Metropole, a meeting of the Party's Central Committee is in progress.

> FOLLOWING THE DEATH OF MIRBACH[1] THE GERMANS WANT TO SEND 5,000 SOLDIERS INTO MOSCOW.

An ill and exhausted Lenin reads the Council of People's Commissars' Resolution.

Tired members of the Central Committee accept the decision without argument.

> WE REFUSE.

The gun turrets on the German battleship *Geben* swing in to aim.

An officer in the gleaming helmet awaits the reply of the officer in the straw hat.

> STOP AT ONCE. SURRENDER ARMS, GRAIN AND FODDER, AND AWAIT FURTHER INSTRUCTIONS.

Even had he wanted to execute the German commander's order, the officer could not have done so.

No officer could have held back the mass of two hundred thousand people flowing like lava down the mountainside.

But the officer did not even consider " wanting " to obey.

He returned the order to the officer in the helmet.

A German cutter carried the refusal back to the battleship.

The lava pouring down the mountains flowed along the road twisting down the Black Sea shore.

The German commander waited, precisely according to his watch.

The lava flow did not cease.

The quick-firing guns of the battleship fired a salvo.

The shells fell short,

but they terrified the horses.

A stallion reared onto its hind legs, smashing the shafts.

Some twenty people grabbed at his nostrils, ears, tail, legs and mane,

---

[1] Count von Mirbach, the German Ambassador to Moscow, was killed in Moscow on July 6, 1918, by Social-Revolutionaries anxious to provoke new hostilities with Germany.

163

dragging him into a ditch. They pulled the shattered wagon into the ditch and the chain of carts moved on without a pause.

The German commander waited a little longer . . . and then turned the muzzles of the 12-inch guns.

The guns blasted, throwing out clouds of black smoke.

The shells fell into the thick of the crowd, flinging a wagon **and** horses into the air with their load of people and pillows.

Fragments and slivers were all that fell back onto the ground.

The terrified horses bolted.

Crazed with fear, women and children started to shriek, spreading panic around them.

The shells fell steadily and accurately.

Cows, horses and people began to drop.

The cries of the wounded were disregarded — they were gathered up and flung into the wagons.

The carts stuck in the ruts and people lashed the bellies and backs of the horses with whips, crutches, shovels and sticks.

The maddening pain either felled the horses on the spot or sent them into a crazed gallop across the pathless stones.

The carts spun behind them, spilling out children, mirrors, wounded, pillows and Singer sewing machines.

Whatever fell out was immediately crushed under the wheels and hooves and the feet of the fear-crazed, stampeding mass of people.

The path twisted behind a tall cliff.

The shells ceased to find their targets.

Miraculously, the commander of the Red units was able to turn the artillery.

Six guns were aimed towards the sea.

One gun couldn't be stopped because its entire crew was dead, and the horses, with no one at the reins, careered across the stony shore without a backward glance.

The six guns fired a volley, but only two shells left the guns.

The remainder had been ruined.

Two 3-inch shells splashed into the water, exploding far away from the ship at anchor.

The German commander turned red with rage and signalled to the shore.

Two hydroplanes, with German crosses on their wings, took to the air.

Where the ship's cannon could not reach, the bombs of the hydroplanes did.

The flow of people had barely calmed down and now it panicked with new frenzy.

The six guns had to be abandoned.

The commanding officer could do nothing with the captains. The captains were powerless over their sections.

JUST TO GET AWAY!

Was the thought in everyone's eyes and hearts.
No one gathered up the wounded anymore.
No one waited for the weak anymore.
The fallen were no longer given time to pick themselves up.
The writhing, living chain was clearly visible from the aircraft, and so was the road that swiftly opened up behind them, littered with patches of different colour.
The patches were pillows, mirrors, sewing machines and bits of wagons and horses.
They were the remains of trampled people, the bodies of slaughtered children.
Night came on.
The battleship's searchlights were turned on.
Apart from the lifeless remains of the lava flow that had gushed through that way, the searchlights picked out nothing more.
In the pre-dawn mist,
The shattered chain of carts moved on

TO JOIN THE RED ARMIES,

not stopping even for a minute, pausing just long enough to water the horses.

In Moscow, poster after poster goes up, stuck with paste that has hardened in the cold.

MOBILISATION OF THE PARTY!
MOBILISATION OF THE TRADE UNIONS!
GENERAL MOBILISATION!
TO THE FRONT! TO THE FRONT! TO THE FRONT!

The Bolshoi Theatre is surrounded by machine-guns, mobile kitchens and fires.
In the theatre — a meeting is in progress.
An old peasant who has survived three tsars is in the chair.
Speakers, resolutions, announcements.

FUEL AND COAL ARE IN THE HANDS OF THE WHITES.

Special announcements:

THE MENSHEVIKS HAVE SEIZED POWER IN GEORGIA.

Under the command of their elegant officers — the princes of Georgia — troops were fortifying the approaches to the piece of land occupied by the Mensheviks.

A Georgian patrol defending a bridge across a deep ravine had established its camp on an inaccessible crag.

The front lines of the stream of people fleeing the merciless Cossacks

TO UNITE WITH THE RED ARMIES

came under fire from the Georgian machine-guns.

Gunfire ahead.

Agitation in the column.

The officers and soldiers dashed ahead, leaping out of the carts and away from the women and children.

The survivors of the front lines galloped up to report to the commanding officer.

The officers reached their conclusion.

IF WE RETREAT — IT'S DEATH ON COSSACK SABRES
IF WE GO FORWARD — IT'S DEATH UNDER GEORGIAN MACHINE GUNS AND RIFLES.
IF WE STOP AND WAIT HERE — IT'S DEATH FROM COLD AND HUNGER.

The stream froze in painful expectation between the two cliffs which hemmed them in like walls.

In the Georgian camp the gramophone was playing — because the inaccessible position guaranteed their safety.

The spirits of the Red officers sank, because every way out of the situation spelled real death.

REVOLUTION AND SOCIALISM

was written on the flags.

Death and destruction lay around.

Despair was written on the faces and in the eyes of the exhausted people.

Suddenly, bedraggled scouts returned with shrewd smiles on their faces.

The scouts outlined their plan in excited whispers.

The inaccessible crags,

the bridge which could not be crossed because of the machine-gun post,

the calm confidence reigning in the camp

— all plunged swiftly into the southern night.

Not a sound, not a light in the gorge where thousands of people were huddled together.

The captains gave commands in whispers.

Feeling their way in the darkness, the Red units crept towards the Georgian encampment.

They scaled the sheer rock face, climbing on each other's shoulders, grasping for holds and branches of scrubs.

Thrusting poles into the crevices in the rock for support, a thousand sun-baked, unshaven people,
in torn and dusty clothes,
clambered upwards in unbroken silence,
making their way along the inaccessible wall towards the rear of the Georgian ambush.

The Georgians were overwhelmed by the superhuman energy, the unbounded courage and fearless daring of people who were ready to die for liberty.

The Georgians took flight,
making their escape in boats which carried them to ships.

Smoke poured out of the ships' funnels and they sailed off.

A great many shells were abandoned in the Georgian camp,
and sixteen guns,
field kitchens,
a small store of fodder,
and a gramophone and records.

Cooked food was also left behind.

The partisans flung themselves on the food like hungry dogs.

People scraped up the remains of food from the pots of the field kitchens.

Children gathered up the last crumbs of bread.

Artillery horses shared their fodder with the cows from the wagon train.

A sudden gale blew up.

Suddenly, clouds started to gather.

Black clouds hid the snowy peaks and then burst into a torrential downpour.

Muddy rivers of water rushed down from the mountains,
washing away stones and trees in their path.

The water gushed down the mountain road as if it were a convenient river bed.

In a few moments the road was transformed into a turbulent mountain river.

The great mass of water rushed down and hit the slipping column of carts, submerging people up to their knees and the wheels up to the axles.

People clutched at each other to avoid being washed off their feet into the ravine.

They grabbed at the carts, at the horses and at protruding rocks and

167

roots of scrubs.

The torrential rain soaked them to the skin, drenched the canvas covering on the wagons, and soaked all the pillows and blankets.

The downpour gathered force.

The muddy rivers rushing down the mountain grew stronger.

Chutes of water gushed down from the ledges.

Between the ravine and the sheer rock face, washed by jets of muddy water, drowned in the rushing currents, battered by winds, the partisans, women and children fought with superhuman strength against the maddened elements.

The onslaught intensified.

Water jetted off the edge of the roadway into the ravine dragging things with it.

The water conquered the veteran forces of one old man and carried him into the ravine.

A wagon rolled backwards until its rear wheels slipped over the edge and, spinning around with its horses and passengers, it disappeared into the ravine.

The artillery horses strained themselves to breaking point trying to hold back the guns against the pressure of water beating against the sheet-metal.

Step by step, the horses gave way before the onslaught.

Step by step, the wheels of the gun carriages edged nearer the precipice.

Suddenly a fresh chute of water jetted down from above, hitting the road with tremendous force.

The horses took fright and shied backwards.

Two guns overturned onto their tails and spun down the steep stone face, dragging the horses with them.

The cavalrymen rushed up, straining every muscle to hold back the horses which could not comprehend the danger.

One after another, men were washed downwards, dragged away by the current.

The black clouds grew denser, till they shut out all light.

In the growing darkness, gaunt, sun-blackened people fought like animals, like demons, against the mounting, elemental force of water.

The approach of night hid the end of that desperate and tragic struggle from sight.

TO JOIN THE RED ARMIES —

the battered stream of thousands which had passed through fire and water, crawled on towards the last pass, never stopping on their way.

Horses which could hold out no longer were dropping in their tracks;

168

people moved their carcasses into the ditch and resumed their ceaseless march.

FOR THE THIRD MONTH

the wheels squealed monotonously.
For the third month, the leg muscles strained.
The wagon train no longer carried young babies, the herd of cows had by now thinned out, and by now it was difficult to find a dog in the column.
Eyes were fixed unblinkingly ahead, still clinging to hope.
And before those eyes, a flock of ravens rose heavily into the air.
The wind brought a smell of putrefaction.
Someone handed the commanding officer a piece of paper taken from a telegraph pole.
Written on it in sun-baked blood was:

SO WILL WE DEAL WITH ALL BOLSHEVIKS
General Stankevich

Five hundred slashed, naked human bodies lay in a hollow.
The commander removed the remnants of his straw hat and, following his example, every one took off the grass and twig covering from his head.
To the strains of the record of an orchestra found in the Georgian camp

THEY BURIED THEIR SLAUGHTERED COMRADES.

A dynamite charge brought down the rock face.
The tumbling stones showered down on that vast and extraordinary grave.
The fragments of rock piled up into a mountain, in the form of a massive monument.
On the flat side of a huge slab these words appeared:

YOU HAVE KILLED PEOPLE.
WE SHALL DESTROY CLASSES.

And with a shudder, the suffering, mangled column moved off

TO JOIN THE RED ARMIES.

Through the bare, uninhabited steppe,
with pain in their hearts and tears in their eyes — leaving their un-harvested fields and the rich black earth of the Kuban further and further behind.
They passed weathered skeletons of camels — omens of hunger and desolation.
Out of the Caucasian mountain range into

169

the endless steppes, in the face of leaden, winter clouds.

Act Eight

The air was wrapped in a thick sheet of icy fog which hid the end of the snows and the beginning of the sky.
The endless, sombre chain of carts and partisans crawled into the boundless, snow-covered wilderness.
The column carried three flags.
Three blackened flags, scorched at the edges, riddled with bullets and worn to rags.
On one: Long live Socialism!
On another: Astrakhan Division.
On another: some unknown words in Turkic.
Three broken armies had merged into one.
But those three armies together made less people than there had originally been in one.[1]
Tartars and Turkmen had mingled with the Kuban cavalry.
Winding among the horses and oxen were camels, laden with wounded Turkic fighters. Donkeys, trembling with cold, moved slowly on.
A north wind blew ceaselessly across the steppe.
The snow stuck to the wheels.
The wheels stuck in the deep snow drifts.
The men and beasts strained themselves to breaking point, pushing onwards step by step.
Clouds of steam rose over their sweating bodies like a fog.
But not everyone was sweating — only those who had the strength to keep moving and those whose temperature had been pushed beyond the limit by typhoid.
Those who — from exhaustion, hunger or typhoid — could no longer walk, lay in the carts, huddling close to one another for warmth, covering themselves in the remaining pieces of clothing, pillows and blankets. The wind tore at the white roofs of the wagons, cold crept in through all the cracks.
Emaciated bodies, whitened by fever, trembled like the string of a violin.
The column moved on without stopping.

---

[1] After the Taman Army had joined up with the main Soviet forces in the Southern Caucasus in the autumn of 1918, the intensive battle with the White Cossacks continued. Under pressure from the Cossacks, the Soviet armies in the Southern Caucasus were soon obliged to make their way towards Astrakhan through the Kalmuk steppes. This was the beginning of the so-called "Astrakhan march" which is in fact described in Act 8 of the script.

It moved stubbornly on, unable to stop.

It could not stop because it would have stiffened up and frozen in an hour, and in a week, would have been buried without trace under the snow.

That was why the stream moved on without halting

TO JOIN THE RED ARMY FORCES.

And the Red Army forces? Straining itself to the limit, with unprecedented endurance, the young Red Army is holding back the White forces pressing in from all sides.

ORDER OF THE MILITARY-REVOLUTIONARY COMMITTEE:
REMEMBER THAT THE FATE OF THE WORKING CLASS AND THE PEASANTRY, THE FATE OF THE NATION AS A WHOLE, AND OF A LONG LINE OF FUTURE GENERATIONS, DEPENDS ON YOUR STAND, YOUR FIRMNESS AND YOUR DISCIPLINE.

And the Red Army men bear this firmly in mind.

And the Red Army men stand firm in the ranks of the fighting armies.

More and more appeals go up in the towns.

TO THE FRONT! TO THE FRONT! TO THE FRONT!

More and more workers' units are leaving Moscow, and they listen to a parting speech from the platform in Theatre Square.[1]

THE RED ARMY FIGHTER IS GIVEN ARMS TO DEFEND THE WORKERS FROM THE EXPLOITER, THE LANDOWNER AND THE CAPITALIST.

Convoy after convoy leaves the railway station loaded with soldiers.

At the front, commissars address the newly-arriving units:

IN THE NAME OF THE REVOLUTION, WE DEMAND OF EACH AND ALL OF YOU, NOT JUST FIRMNESS AND ENDURANCE, BUT SELFLESS HEROISM.

The White Guard's shells whistle, the enemy regiments move in.

The Red Army holds on to its position with all its strength, but slowly it begins to fall back, battling over every inch of ground yielded.

---

[1] What the authors seem to have in mind here is the famous speech by V. I. Lenin given on the occasion of the departure of the Red Armies for the front. Chronologically, however, it took place considerably later.

Through gale and snowstorm, clambering out of the snow-filled hollows, straining its forces to the utmost, never halting at night, never pausing for a moment, the stream of people pressed on.

More and more frequently, cows, horses and oxen drop from hunger.

Their frozen carcasses were flung to one side and the stream flowed on without pausing.

More and more frequently, wagons fall behind, left without horses.

They fall behind and stand alone in the snowy gale, in the stinging cold and in the impassive ocean of snow.

Another wagon has fallen behind.

An emaciated woman pulls out two half-dead children from under the heap of rags in the wagon.

While two more half-dead children are left to freeze — the mother does not have enough arms for them.

The persistent wind blows, and the storm whirls around them.

The last of the carts are leaving.

The mother leaves the other children behind.

She does not cry, she walks, dry-eyed.

She has no more tears to shed.

She herself is as withered as a skeleton.

The frost grows sharper. The wind intensifies. It buries everything that stands still in the steppe under the snow.

Raking away the snow drifts with shovels, planks, sticks, and the butts of rifles, the stream cleared a way through the endless snows.

Their path led them through a poor Astrakhan village.

The frozen people flung themselves at the snow-covered doors of the houses.

They beat on the doors, shouted, begged and prayed for them to open.

But the doors remained shut.

The endless chain of wagons crawled through the village — people were afraid of death and dying, of freezing to death.

They wanted to warm themselves for a few moments and that was why they beat at the doors.

But the doors remained shut. Sensing the approach of death, people knocked louder, shouted and wept.

But the doors remained stubbornly shut. There was no one who could have opened the doors — all the peasants lay in a fever of typhus.

A sick Tartar gathered all his energies in an effort to crawl over to open the door. All night the ailing peasants could hear the squeal of wheels on the frozen snow.

All night the human lava flowed through the terrifyingly deserted village. Just before morning, the Tartar managed to reach the door and pull back

the latch with his feeble, bony hand, before losing consciousness.
A wild wind blew open the door. . . .
Near the doorway lay the bodies of two who had feared dying.
The wind ruffled their hair.
The wind tore the tarpaulins on the abandoned wagons.
The wind swept the snow over the mournful traces left by that stream of people.
Frozen camels stood like black idols, staring into the snow-filled distance with wide, glassy eyes.
The stream flowed into the distance, leaving behind a path trodden down in the snow, strewn with the corpses of people and animals.
The overloaded wagons were filled with people delirious from typhus.
The village they left behind lay in the grip of typhus.

> THE WHOLE OF SOVIET RUSSIA WAS IN THE GRIP OF TYPHUS.

Railway stations turned sick bays, convoys of typhoid victims.
Frost, storm, darkness.
Never ceasing their onward march, the partisan forces pressed forward

> TO JOIN THE RED ARMIES.

The Red Army, carrying out the orders of the Military-Revolutionary Committee, is stretching its forces to the limit.
On wheels,
on foot,
in sleds,
on horseback,
The Red front pushes on unceasingly!

> EVERY MOMENT GAINED BY US SAVES TOWNS, THOUSANDS OF WORKERS' LIVES, AND MILLIONS' WORTH OF NATIONAL PROPERTY.

Order after order:

> REMEMBER: THE TASK OF THE RED ARMY IS NOT TO CONQUER THE LAND, BUT TO LIBERATE IT.

> STRIVING TO BREAK THROUGH ENEMY LINES TO JOIN UP WITH THE MILLIONS OF RED PARTISAN FIGHTERS

The Red Army breaks through one encirclement after another, with legendary courage.

173

With selfless heroism it holds back the ninth wave of the counter-revolution:

EVERYTHING THAT WOULD CRUSH FREEDOM.

English guns,
German battleships,
Serbian heavy artillery,
Polish dragoons,
the Czechs,
the Japanese,
the Don Cossacks,
the black colonial armies,
the generals,
the Mensheviks —

EVERYTHING THAT WOULD STRANGLE THE SOVIETS. . . .

Teeth clenched,
guns firmly grasped, the Red Army is guarding the line of trenches along the Soviet front.
Their eyes pierce the dark night.
But nature is indifferent.
Nature sees neither death nor blood.
Nature has wrapped the bushes and trees in hoar frost, and now play-fully displays the beauties of the winter night.
Fields of white sparks glitter on the surface of the snows.
Large stars glimmer in the sky.
The Red sentries stand motionless in the still night.
The cold muzzles of machine guns stare out at the snowy hillock.
The eyes of the Soviet soldiers stare out through the darkness in the direction of the enemy.
Tired men sink towards the snow.
Their eyes drop.
Their muscles slacken.
But suddenly through sleep's drowsy embrace, through the stillness of that quiet night, comes the sound of singing.
It must be a hallucination.
Sounds float in through the darkness.

LORD, SAVE. . . .

What can it mean?
Heads are raised. . . .
Eyes open. . . .

LORD, SAVE THY PEOPLE . . .

floats in over the white plain.

AND BLESS THINE INHERITANCE. . . .

From the distance — visible in the light of the winter moon, a strange crowd flows in.
glittering with gold brocade,
surrounded by the bright lights of lamps and candles.
Agitation and activity breaks out in the trenches.
What can it mean?
I don't know.
What should we do?
We'll have to see what it is.
Bewilderment shows on the faces of the Red Army fighters.
Nearer and nearer.
Now they can be seen clearly.
Icons, banners, crosses, censers.
Priests dressed in their ritual attire, in dazzling cassocks.
Behind their front column comes a dense crowd of burly, black-robed monks.
Those in front are carrying crosses and waving smoking censers.

LORD, SAVE THY PEOPLE.

Nearer and nearer.
The Red Army men rush around the trenches. It's obvious that they are very recently from the village.
It's obvious that they are anxious and bewildered.

WHAT'S TO BE DONE?

Only a few paces now separate the advancing crowd from the trenches.

AND BLESS THINE INHERITANCE.

A scout rushes up to a dug-out:

COMRADE COMMISSAR. . . .

Without waiting to hear him out, the commissar runs to the trenches.
Jumping onto the breastwork, and seeing what is happening, he understands.

HALT.

The procession halts.

175

The priests leave off their chanting.
The monks clench their teeth and narrow their eyes.
The commissar strides forward.
Suddenly, from under a chasuble, the flash of gold braid.
Suddenly the glittering front column parts.
And as they part, they reveal a line of bayonets and a chain of machine guns.
The Red Army men don't have time to run up.
They don't have time to wake up properly.
The monks' rifles spit out a shower of lead.
Riddled with bullets, the commissar falls back into the trench.
Frenzied firing breaks out from the priests' machine guns.
The Red Army fighters shudder with the unexpectedness of it.

THE ARMY OF JESUS CHRIST

launches a crushing attack on the trenches.
Like animals, the long-haired monks and priests fling themselves on the duped soldiers of the Red Army.
They slash, stab and shoot.
The captains cannot establish any order.
The Red Army forces flee in panic.
Cossack cavalry dashes out from behind the hillock and finishes off the business begun by the priests.
Artillery — tanks — an armoured train — bring up fresh forces.
The Red Army begins to retreat.

SEVEN DAYS LATER

the stream of people reached the trenches abandoned in the flight.

THE RED ARMY IS CLOSE AT HAND.

The exhausted partisans took heart.
They gathered all the horses which were still firm on their feet,

THEY SENT THE CAVALRY ON AHEAD.

In thickly falling snow
they bade the departing unit farewell on their prancing horses.
The vanguard galloped off in the steps of the retreating army.
The commanding officer led the stream after them.

Meanwhile news reached Moscow:

A 4,000-STRONG ARMY OF PARTISANS HAS PERISHED ON

176

THE SHORES OF THE BLACK SEA BY THE SWORDS OF THE COSSACKS. THE SURVIVORS FROZE TO DEATH IN THE ASTRAKHAN STEPPES, TO THE LAST MAN.

To verify this information

THE PARTY CENTRAL COMMITTEE

sent a plane out from the aerodrome.
The vanguard of the stream, fighting off the White units, was catching up with the retreating Red Army.
The plane fell into a snowstorm, rolled over and crashed into the snowy steppes.
The snowstorm swept away the traces of the wreck.
No news came to the Central Committee.

On a clear, icy day, the advance lines of the stream caught sight of soldiers standing in the distance.
The officers in command gave the battle order to the reserve troops.
The stream drew closer.
The soldiers did not fire.

THEY'RE NOT FIRING!

Faces brightened, eyes shone.

THEY'RE OURS!

At last! People rushed out to meet them.

THEY'RE REDS!
REDS!
REDS!

A man from Kuban circled uncomprehendingly around a motionless Red Army man.
The soldier stood like stone in his snow-covered helmet.
A thousand Red Army men stood like that, stricken by the frost.

THEY HAD FROZEN TO DEATH.

They stood leaning against hay ricks.
Squatting on their haunches.
They stood in groups, huddled close to one another.
Their faces were paper-white.
Their hands like white wax.
All were covered by the snow.

The horses, cows and camels immediately threw themselves on the hay.
The spirits of a thousand partisans fell.
Evening was coming on.
People set the hay alight to warm their frozen hands and feet.
The frozen figures of the soldiers stood like mummies in the approaching twilight.
In the flickering firelight their faces seemed to be twisting into terrible grimaces.
From the outside, it was a fearful sight.
The steppe, the twilight and the fires;
skeleton-like people warming themselves in front of the fires;
the figures transfixed by the frost standing as motionless as statues;
terrifying shadows cast by the flames dancing over the white snow.
A woman caught sight of a face — glassy eyes and bared teeth — shrieked and fled, beside herself with terror.
The woman's cry struck everyone like a whiplash.
Instantly everyone broke away and rushed off.
Carts, camels, cows,
women and old people,
they dashed away in the grip of a deathly fear which had overcome them suddenly.
A snowstorm was brewing.
The frost-stricken figures
of the Red Army soldiers
stood as if on sentry duty.

Act Nine

The " black circle " around Moscow is shrinking. The RSFSR now consists solely of the territory covered by the province of Moscow.[1]

> IN THE SITUATION WHICH HAS ARISEN FOR THE COUNTRY, COMMUNISTS CAN HAVE NO ROOM FOR DOUBT, HESITATION, BACKWARD GLANCES, OR CRITICISM — THERE IS ONLY ONE SLOGAN POSSIBLE — FORWARD!

Hungry, ill-clad and filthy, the Soviet troops hold back the onslaught of the enemy forces.

> EVERYTHING FOR THE FRONT!

---

[1] There is clearly a certain amount of exaggeration on the part of the authors here, although they are in fact concerned with the most difficult period of the Civil War — the period in 1919 when the White armies had their greatest successes.

178

Clothing,
bread,
linen,
guns,
boots,
bandages,
bicycles,
lorries,
motorcycles.

IN THE NEXT FEW DAYS WE MUST ENSURE THAT EVERY
SOLDIER IS FED, CLOTHED, SHOD AND ARMED.

That's why young communists and women workers go the rounds of the
houses collecting something from every home, a shirt, a piece of bandage,
a pound of flour, a few ounces of sugar.
That's why women workers are urgently stitching up the seams of warm
jerseys.
That's why the townspeople are going out on vast " working holidays "
and chopping down forests and parks, sawing wood, loading convoys
and clearing the railway lines of snow.
That's why the horses of cab drivers, peasants and draymen are being
mobilised.
That's why a new poster shouts:

PROLETARIAN, TO HORSE.

This is in Moscow — in the city centre.
Meanwhile in the outlying districts. . . .
In the steppes the tenacious partisan army received

AN ULTIMATUM FROM GENERAL KRASNOV.
YOU DAMNED SCOUNDRELS . . . BEAR IN MIND THAT THE
END IS AT HAND FOR THE BOLSHEVIKS.
YOU CAN GO NO FURTHER BECAUSE YOU ARE SUR-
ROUNDED BY MY ARMIES. IF YOU WANT TO BE SPARED,
SURRENDER ALL YOUR OFFICERS AND GIVE UP YOUR
WEAPONS. IF YOU DON'T SURRENDER, I WILL RUB EVERY
LAST ONE OF YOU OFF THE FACE OF THE EARTH.

Worn down to their bones, famished and frozen, the partisans heard out
the General's fury sombrely.
They realised the lack of alternative. . . .
Despair overwhelmed them all.
They all bowed their heads under the weight of bitterness that welled

179

up in them.

The wind whirled up the snow.

The snow-covered steppes stretched endlessly around.

The partisan leaders said without agitation or heat:

> NOW . . . THAT YOU KNOW THE TRUTH, ACT ACCORDING TO THE DICTATES OF YOUR CONSCIENCES AND THE DEMANDS OF YOUR OWN INTERESTS.

A silence of the grave, an elemental despair, hung over the still crowd of thousands.

Suddenly, one man pricked up his ears. Then more and more raised their heads.

A thousand ears turned towards a single point.

A thousand chests stopped breathing.

Somewhere far away a shell burst.

Guns rang out.

Dozens of bombs exploded.

The crowd surged like feathers before the wind.

Everyone leapt to his feet.

Everyone started grabbing whatever was to hand, poles, shovels, planks, switches, reins, daggers, rifles, stones, crutches,

all — women, children, the wounded, the ill and the aged —

all rushed in one direction.

On horses, cows and oxen — the partisan cavalry dashed off.

THE REMOUNT STATION

The Red regiments were falling back under the pressure of the Cossacks.

The Red regiments in retreat came up against a swift-flowing river.

The partisans struck at the Cossacks' rear guard with great and unexpected force.

Down the railway line came a train decked out with slogans.

THE FIRST MOSCOW WORKERS' REGIMENT

leapt from its carriages and dashed into attack.

Panic seized the Cossacks.

This time victory was assured for the Red Army forces.

THE FORCES HAD JOINED UP.

Embraces, kisses, handshakes, laughter and tears.

Putting on quilted trousers and tucking into cabbage soup from the field kitchen, the partisans roared unrestrainedly with the joy that overwhelmed them.

Over the bubbling general exultation floated a banner carrying the Red
five-pointed star,
and in its centre, the Hammer and Sickle.

THE PREPARATORY WORK IS OVER.
WE HAVE BROUGHT TOGETHER ALL THE NECESSARY FORCES
AND MEANS
OUR RANKS ARE FORMED
NOW . . .
ON THE SIGNAL,
FORWARD!

And that was where the battle began.
A battle which the written word is inadequate to describe.
A battle which can be told, more or less.
It was the Synthesis.
It was the Gamut.
It was the Kaleidoscope of all the heroic victories of the Red Army.
It was the condensation of the agonising exertion of a whole nation
such as history had never seen, of unprecedented courage, endurance
and heroism.
It was the symbolic confrontation of the proletarian and peasant masses
with the hydra-heads of counter-revolution.
A confrontation in which people fought as if possessed.
In which the legendary valour of the fighters and of whole armies reached
ultimate limits.
Lead, steel, fire.
Thunder, lightning.
Explosions, blasts and the crunching chop of cavalry.
The synthesis of all the splendid victories achieved by the mightiest
of all victories.
The battle of Perekop!
A victory which razed the forces of counter-revolution to the ground.

AND THEN —

The cavalry men hitched their horses to the ploughshare and the harrow.
The workers took up their posts.
And the lever of Soviet history was
switched sharply over to
peaceful construction.

181

3. Alexander Nevsky

Final scenes of an earlier version of the script.

Early spring in Pereyaslavl. Boats on the shores of the lake.
The princess, with children already in their teens, is saying goodbye to
her husband. Around them is a crowd of peasants on their way to battle.
The Prince is thinner, maturer, and he is reserved. His character is not
what it was in former times. He is no longer the cheerful army commander, but a wise and wary politician and manager.
*Make ready the boats! When I return from the Golden Horde, the fight-
ing will begin,* he tells old Alexander. *I entrust my wife, my children and
my lands to your care!*

The Golden Horde again. Sultry heat. Noise. Shrill songs. The neighing
of a thousand head of horses. The Golden Horde is expecting the Russian
Prince. Signs of tension are evident. The princelings Ivanko and Vasilko,
who are wearing Chinese robes with scimitars at their waists, are more
restlessly active than the rest.
He's coming! a rider brings word. All activity dies in the stalls in front
of the tent.
Light the fires! the master of ceremonies spurs on the princes. *You shall
see what you shall see!*
Behind the stalls, the executioner quickly prepares the block. The crowd
runs in from all sides. Horses, children. Tall mongolian hats. They wait.
Alexander rides up with a small retinue. It includes familiar faces —
Pelgusy, Nikita, Mikhalka. The Prince is dressed as for battle — an
awe-inspiring figure. A deathly hush comes over the crowd as the Prince
dismounts. The fires flare up.
The Khan's emissary tells him:
Pass between the fires — you must purify yourself!
Alexander looks at the crowd. He sees the faces of Ivanko and Vasilko,
sees that they are drawing daggers under their robes, and calmly he
walks between the fires. Alexander's agreement takes the crowd by
surprise, they break into a hubbub and then immediately fall silent again.
Ivanko and Vasilko approach the Prince who barely gives any sign of
recognition. His face is pale and wet with perspiration.
Take off your helmet, unbuckle your sword! they tell him.
He clenches his teeth and silently gives up his helmet and sword.
Everyone feels a sense of anti-climax. The princelings exchange glances,
not knowing what to make of it. Alexander stands alone in the open
space before the tent. The smiling old master of ceremonies, who has
seen many things in China in his time, goes up to him quickly:

Now, kneel down before the tent, you will be received as a guest! he says, his eyes seeking the princelings. They are standing alongside, their hands in the bosoms of their robes. Their faces mirror a firm conviction that Alexander is now lost. Alexander's face grows even colder and more frightening. He goes down on his knees.

The crowd roars with delight. *Aha! he's on his knees!* The curtain of the tent is drawn back and the Khan beckons his guest to sit down beside him. The tent is in half-darkness. The Khan and his senior wife are seated on soft cushions sewn with pearls. Behind them are the ministers, military leaders, advisers and both the fugitive Russian princes.

Alexander sits on a saddle thrown down on the carpet before the Khan's seat. The Khan looks at him silently and Alexander's eyes meet his unwaveringly. On his finger he wears the ring received as a gift.

The princes bring complaint against you, says the Khan. Alexander is silent.

You take all honour to yourself, you give them nothing, Alexander is silent.

I am not envious, however, the Khan continues, but Alexander is silent as before. *Gather the people, make war if you so wish.* Alexander is silent still.

I will give you 100,000 horsemen. Alexander is silent.

He's lost! the princelings whisper.

A different thought lies on my heart, Khan, Alexander suddenly begins.
What thought is that, Iskander?

To rule over the Russian domain.

The princelings slap their thighs in indignation.

It is I who rule Rus, Iskander.

Caught up in some deep and secret thought, Alexander shakes his head. *To every house, its own mouse,* he says. *It does not become me to abandon my heritage.*

At that the princelings lose all restraint.

He is plotting against you, Great Khan! shouts Ivanko.

You've beaten the Germans, and now you want the Golden Horde . . . shouts Vasilko.

Is that what you want? Khan Barkai asks softly, his eyes narrowing.

His wife has meanwhile signalled with her eyes to the doctor standing in a corner of the tent: he pours something into a helmet, smearing it over the inside surface. It is something he himself is afraid to touch.

The Khan's wife indicates approval with her eyes and the Khan too has observed this episode.

Is it? he reiterates to Alexander.

I want what Rus wants, Khan. If Rus sends me against you — I will go.

Shouting breaks out. The Khan rises to his feet. All freeze, all lower their heads. Alexander rises also to his feet. The two giants stand face to face, staring fixedly at each other.

The princelings smile greedily. It's all over, They unsheath their knives. *I like brave men*, says the Khan. *Return to your home!* and he sits down. *You shall be the commander there. It is not fitting that we quarrel with you*, he says, smiling a thin smile.

Alexander leaves. Cowed, Ivanko and Vasilko kiss the edge of his cloak and hand him his sword and helmet.

Honour and glory to you, Prince! Honour and glory! they mumble.

Alexander kicks them away without a word. The Mongols laugh.

Alexander and his retinue gallop home to Rus. They halt at a stopping place by a river. Alexander is flushed and agitated. Pelgusy tells him:

Well Prince, I did not think — I would never have foretold that the affair would turn out this way. You have gained a victory. The Khan has shown you great respect!

Alexander takes off his helmet.

Dip me some water to drink in this, he tells Mikhalka.

As he thirstily gulps down the cold water he replies to Pelgusy:

More evil than evil is the respect of the Tartar, my brother!

But the water is foul-tasting. He flings the rest from his helmet without drinking it.

And they mount up again.

To Rus, with all speed! says Alexander. *Rus is lying prone, we must raise her to her feet!*

The rivers stretch by, fields fly past. Autumn. The heavy mud makes the going difficult. Ravaged villages, unharvested fields, hungry dogs, bones of old battles — they have entered Rus.

Alexander and his retinue take off their helmets as they pass through the relics of battles.

Ryazan fought here! Alexander says, looking at the bones.

Here Suzdal laid down its life. At another spot. . . .

The Prince is ill. His face is sallow and worn. But he does not wish to rest.

Home! Home! he urges on his attendants. *Give no thought to the pain. There is much to be done. The time has come to attack the Golden Horde.*

But by now he can no longer sit in the saddle. He is carried in a litter between two saddles.

I must go on! On! To rouse Rus! he mutters. *So, they have poisoned me, the dogs. . . . On!*

And one day his strength goes altogether. His guard spread cloaks and horse cloths on the ground and lay the Prince down on them. He is barely breathing. The monks of a poor, depleted cloister in the neighbourhood invite him in. Pelgusy is ready to agree, but Alexander hears and motions with his hand.

We must go on! . . . Turn off nowhere! and he sinks back into delirium. *We shall not be free of the Golden Horde while Rus lies prone. Rus must be brought to her feet!*

Are we really to attack the Golden Horde, Prince? asks Mikhalka.

Alexander raises himself on his elbow and looks around at the autumn fields of Rus.

This is where we shall fight — a good field, a joyous one! . . . and he falls back dead.

A mournful bell rings out in the cloisters. Peasants gather.

Pelgusy, historian and chronicler by calling, is already writing something on a piece of birch bark.

What place is this? he asks the peasants.

The field of Kulikovo, they tell him.

Alexander's guard wrap his body in a cloak, fix it to some spears and they lift him onto their shoulders.

They ford the rivers. At last the Volga!

Ivan Danilovich Sadko's boat is sailing upstream towards Novgorod. Barge-haulers are singing.

The Prince is back from the Golden Horde! says Sadko. *The affair with the Khan did not end in blows!*

They pass the Oka and overtake Persian boats.

The Khan likes to make his guests welcome, a Persian says enigmatically.

They overtake caravans from India.

This dead man will live long, says an Indian merchant.

Peasants carry the Prince on their shoulders. They carry him across the Russian land, passing him from one shoulder to the next, to the united strains of a song once sung in the snows:

Arise, people of Rus!

. . . hands, and more hands! They rise in the air, but they no longer bear the body of the dead Prince. Instead they carry the banners of Dmitri Donskoi.

The armies of Moscow stand with their moulded, gilded cuirasses, helmets and shields glinting in the sun.

This is where we shall fight — a good field, a joyous one! . . . says the Prince of Moscow, grandson of the long dead Alexander.

He glances up at a banner which bears the image of Alexander and says:

Grandfather and Prince. In your name! . . . and gives the signal to the army.

This is not impoverished Pereyaslavl which has now risen against the Horde.

Moscow has brought together the forces of Rus. A flock of arrows whines through the air on its way to meet the Russians. Leaves drop from the trees. The Tartars charge and scatter.

The heavy Russian wedge silently carves through the Tartar horde. The Tartars flee. The small, gaunt Mamai, watching the battle from a burial mound, leaps onto his horse and shouts something thin, terrible and final.

After him the whole stream of horses gallops off towards the steppes, disappearing into them like a mirage.

4. Casts and Credits

Potemkin (The Battleship Potemkin) (1925)

Produced by Goskino, Moscow. First shown at the 1905 celebrations at the Bolshoi Theatre, Moscow, December 21, 1925; first public screening at the Goskino cinema on Arbat Square, Moscow, December 28, 1925; released in the RSFSR January 18, 1926; 5 reels, 1,740 metres. Scenario by Eisenstein, from an outline by Nina Agadzhanova-Shutko and Eisenstein (*The Year 1905*). Directed by Eisenstein, assisted by Grigori Alexandrov. Photographed by Edward Tisse. Direction assistants: Alexander Antonov, Mikhail Gomarov, Alexander Lyovshin, Maxim Strauch. Group manager: Yakov Bliokh. Sub-titles by Nikolai Aseyev and Sergei Tretyakov. Cast: sailors of the Black Sea Fleet of the Red Navy, citizens of Odessa, members of the Proletkult Theatre, Moscow; and

Vakulinchuk	Alexander Antonov
Chief Officer Gilerovsky	Grigori Alexandrov
Captain Golikov	Vladimir Barsky
Petty Officer	Alexander Lyovshin
humiliated sailor	I. Bobrov
officer on piano	Andrei Fait
Student Fel'dman	Konstantin Feldman
old man	Protopopov
legless veteran	Korobei
lady bringing food to mutineers	Yulia Eisenstein
mother of wounded Aba	Prokopenko
Aba, the wounded boy	A. Glauberman
schoolteacher	N. Poltavtseva
intellectual	Brodsky
student	Zerenin
mother with baby-carriage	Beatrice Vitoldi
militant sailor	Mikhail Gomarov

(Those who played the roles of Matyushenko, ship's doctor Smirnov, the ship's chaplain, and the anti-semite (Glotov?) have not yet been identified.)
Filmed in the city and port of Odessa and in Sevastopol.

October (Ten Days That Shook the World) (1928)

Produced by Sovkino, Moscow. Released January 20, 1928; 7 reels, 2,800 metres. Scenario and direction by Eisenstein and Grigori Alexandrov. Photography by Edward Tisse. Direction assistants: Maxim Strauch, Mikhail Gomarov, Ilya Trauberg. Camera assistants: Vladimir Nilsen, Vladimir Popov. The cast, drawn largely from the people of Leningrad, included

Lenin	V. Nikandrov
Kerensky	N. Popov
Minister Tereshchenko	Boris Livanov
Minister Konovalov	Lyashchenko
Minister Skobelev	Chibisov
Minister Kishkin	Mikholev
Minister Verderevsky	Smelsky
Bolshevik Podvoisky	N. Podvoisky

A reconstruction of the critical days between February and October, 1917, ending on the fall of the Provisional Government. Photographed almost entirely in Leningrad. Known abroad and in America as *Ten Days That Shook the World*.

Alexander Nevsky (1938)

Produced by Mosfilm, Moscow. Released November 23, 1938; 12 reels, 3,044 metres. Scenario by Eisenstein and Pyotr Pavlenko. Directed by Eisenstein, with the collaboration of D. I. Vasiliev. Photographed by Edward Tisse. Music by Sergei Prokofiev. Lyrics by Vladimir Lugovsky. Settings and costumes executed from Eisenstein's sketches by Isaac Shpinel, Nikolai Soloviov, K. Yeliseyev. Sound: B. Volsky, V. Popov. Direction assistants: B. Ivanov, Nikolai Maslov. Camera assistants: S. Uralov, A. Astafiev, N. Bolshakov. Consultant on work with actors: Elena Telesheva. Cast:

Prince Alexander Yaroslavich Nevsky	Nikolai Cherkasov
Vasili Buslai	Nikolai Okhlopkov
Gavrilo Oleksich	Alexander Abrikosov
Ignat, master armourer	Dmitri Orlov
Pavsha, Governor of Pskov	Vasili Novikov
Domash Tverdislavich	Nikolai Arsky
Amelfa Timofeyevna, mother of Buslai	Varvara Massalitinova
Olga, a Novgorod girl	Vera Ivasheva
Vasilisa, a girl of Pskov	Anna Danilova
Von Balk, Grand Master of the Livonian Order	Vladimir Yershov
Tverdilo, traitorous mayor of Pskov	Sergei Blinnikov
Ananias	Ivan Lagutin
The Bishop	Lev Fenin
The Black-robed Monk	Naum Rogozhin

Work on the scenario was begun in the summer of 1937, and the shooting was completed during the summer of 1938. Prokofiev wrote a cantata based on his score, also entitled *Alexander Nevsky*.